Presented to:

FROM

DATE

the Art of Simplicity

A SIMPLE GUIDE TO FOCUSING ON THE ESSENTIALS OF THE HEART

Candy Paull

Stewart, Tabori & Chang
New York

Editor: Marisa Bulzone
Designer: LeAnna Weller Smith
Production Manager: Kim Tyner

Library of Congress Cataloging-in-Publication Data:

Paull, Candy.
The art of simplicity : a simple guide to focusing on the essentials of the heart / by Candy Paull.
p. cm.
Includes bibliographical references (p.).
ISBN 1-58479-447-X
1. Simplicity. 2. Simplicity--Quotations, maxims, etc. I. Title.

BJ1496.P38 2006
179'.9--dc22

2005029808

Published in 2006 by
Stewart, Tabori & Chang
An imprint of
Harry N. Abrams, Inc.

The text of this book was composed in Corporate S, Filosofia and Type Embellishments.

Printed and bound in China by Midas Printing Co., Ltd.
10 9 8 7 6 5 4 3 2 1

HNA
harry n. abrams, inc.
a subsidiary of La Martinière Groupe

Harry N. Abrams, Inc.
115 West 18th Street
New York, NY 10011
www.hnabooks.com

The Art of Simplicity is dedicated to all the unsung heroes
who give the gift of themselves to the world
and
to my dear friend Donna Michael, a wise goddess
who creates beautiful, healing music

contents

INTRODUCTION

Simplicity can be difficult to achieve in a world that clamors for "more! more! more!" But simplicity opens the way to the center of the heart—the place where quiet, healing, and a still small voice await. Simplicity is making elegant choices, treasuring precious moments, and valuing that which is of eternal worth. Like Michelangelo who saw the statue of David in the heart of the stone, so we are called to reveal the inner beauty hidden in the complexity of our lives. Simplicity is singleness of heart, focused on the essentials of life, rather than allowing our desires and fears to distract us. Simplicity is a celebration of the heart—an opportunity to touch eternity in a moment of meditation. Simplicity is finding abundance in the small things and re-discovering the wonder we once knew in the purity of childhood days.

It is my prayer that this little book will inspire you to create a larger life for yourself and for others as you cultivate inner simplicity. May you discover the inner hero hidden within the very nature of your being.

Candy Paull

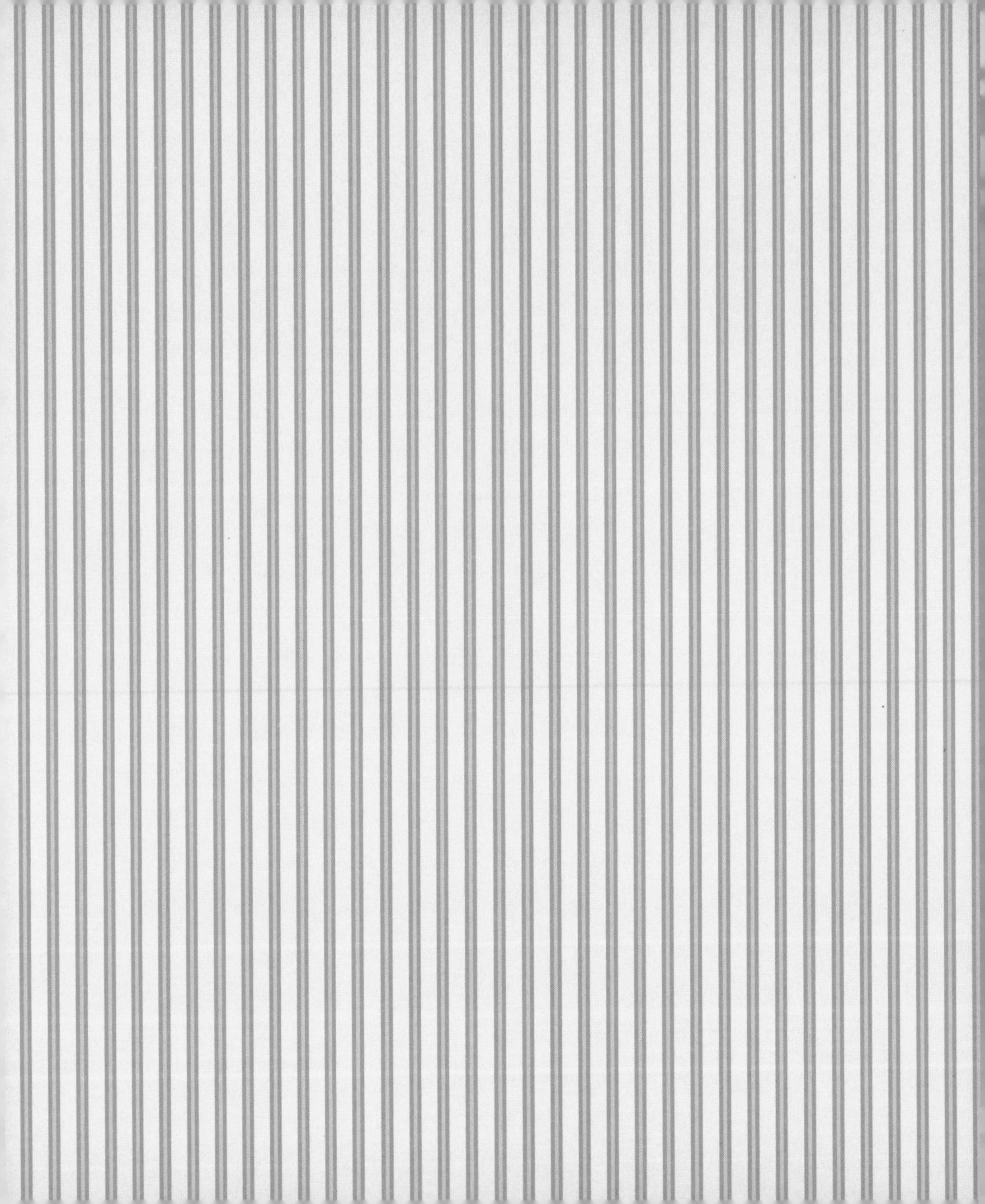

Simplicity Is . . .

For the good man to realize that it is better to be whole than to be good is to enter on a straight and narrow path compared to which his previous rectitude was flowery license.

—JOHN MIDDLETON MURRY

Simplicity is . . . ordering my life around the essentials of the heart.

I think that what we're seeking is an experience of being alive,
so that our life experiences on the purely physical plane will have resonances
within our own innermost being and reality,
so that we actually feel the rapture of being alive.

—JOSEPH CAMPBELL

Simplicity is . . . focusing my attention on what I want to create and experience.

Let us not look back in anger, nor forward in fear,
but around in awareness.

—JAMES THURBER

Simplicity is . . . a single red rose in a crystal vase.

Simplicity is . . . a child's smile.

Simplicity is . . . eyes closed in prayer.

I want to know the mind of God.

The rest is all details

—ALBERT EINSTEIN

The wisdom of life consists in the elimination of nonessentials.

—LIN YUTANG

Simplicity is . . . a moment of silence.

Simplicity is . . . bread, wine, and a table.

Simplicity is . . . a clean closet.

Create in me a clean heart, O God; and renew a right spirit within me.

—PSALM 51:10 (KJV)

The whole thing boils down to giving ourselves in prayer a chance to realize that we have what we seek. We don't have to rush after it. It is there all the time, and if we give it time, it will make itself known to us.

—THOMAS MERTON

Do you have the patience to wait till the mud settles and the water is clear?
Can you remain unmoving till the right action arises by itself?

—TAO TE CHING

Be still and know that I am God.

—PSALM 46:10 (KJV)

The ability to simplify means to eliminate the unnecessary
so that the necessary may speak.

—HANS HOFMANN

Blessed are the pure in heart, for they shall see God.

—MATTHEW 5:8 (RSV)

Simplicity is . . . creating a space for God to enter into my life.
Simplicity is . . . clarity of purpose and purity of heart.

God always takes the simplest way.

—ALBERT EINSTEIN

THE FREEDOM OF SIMPLICITY

It is a spiritual thing to comprehend what simplicity means.

—FRANK LLOYD WRIGHT

The singer opens her mouth and the pure tone floats out freely . . . and its simple beauty goes straight to the heart of the listener and nestles there. You have a gift to offer the world, a song that only you can sing. Like the soprano who has learned to get out of her own way so that her free voice may float on the wings of delight to the listener's ears, you can make choices that empower you to bring the music of your life to a world that needs to receive the gift you bring.

Everyone is born with a song in the heart. Every person has a unique and wonderful gift to give. The pure life potential beats in every heart. And pure potential waits to be expressed.

However, like the soprano who had to learn how to focus and refine her gift so that her true voice could emerge, so you have to clear the way for your unique gift to emerge. *The Art of Simplicity* is written to inspire you to let the one true song of the heart emerge. Sharing wisdom from many sources, a little bit of practical advice, and a few ideas that might spark your thinking, this little guide encourages you to make the changes within that will flow out and transform your outer life. It encourages you to change habits that hold you back and remove the clutter of old beliefs that limit the free expression of the essential you. *The Art of Simplicity* helps you catch a glimpse of your own spiritual magnificence.

This book grew from my own experience of moving into freedom and simplicity. It is an ongoing process. But as I have learned to move beyond victimhood, blame, anger, fear, and all the ego games that held me back, I have discovered that every situation, every choice, every single experience in my life contains the potential for God to work all things together for the highest good and for me to express my unique, one-and-only heartsong in simplicity, love, and joy. I know this can happen for you, too.

No matter what your story, no matter what your past limitations, no matter what mountains must be moved, you have no less potential than any other human being on earth to become the person God created you to be. As you get in touch with the great inner simplicity within, you will see your life re-align itself in miraculous ways. You are a co-creator with God, and even the smallest of choices can change the trajectory of your life, if you are willing to step out in faith.

When your voice is finally free, you become the instrument. All of the events and choices of your life converge in a pure note of joy and peace. You experience the sensation of being at one with the energies of the Universe, a co-creator with God as you release the exquisite song and spin it out into the air. Alive from toes to fingertips, fully present and aware, you sense the life force moving in and through you. And it is beautiful. Because you have focused on the essentials of the heart, your gift is received gladly, for it rises from deep within and touches other hearts at their point of greatest need.

Let your true essence be the goal you seek, and seek to bring that true essence into everything you do—and everything you are. Let the song of love take flight in your life. Come explore the potential and magnificent power that has been buried beneath the clutter and confusion for so long. Enter into the freedom of simplicity.

Become aware of what is in you.
Announce it, pronounce it,
produce it, and give birth to it.

—MEISTER ECKHART

CELEBRATE THE SIMPLE THINGS

I am beginning to learn that it is the sweet, simple things of life which are the real ones after all.

—LAURA INGALLS WILDER

The simple life. Think about what the simple life really means. Does it mean we strip our lives down to the bare bones, give up our homes and our lives for a more ascetic experience? Or can we discover the simplicity that is within the complex lives we already lead?

I believe that simplicity is about focus and choice. In a life full of distractions, it's easy to lose your focus and lose sight of the small simplicities that make up the fabric of everyday existence. These simplicities are the things we tend to pass over and take for granted—at least until some crisis or loss or tragedy takes them from us. Then suddenly we miss the small treasures we took for granted.

The simple things, like clean water or a loving hug or a light in the darkness, are the things that keep us grounded and remind us of our connection to the Life Force. They create a sense of safety and wholeness, cradling us in the here and now of creation. Simple things and simple choices make the difference between merely existing and real living. They are about values and character as much as about material possessions. Whether it is a choice to live life from the heart or a quiet appreciation of the small gifts of life, simple living is about simply living, finding a balance between being and doing, making the most of the life you have been given on earth, right here and right now.

Look at the simple things you enjoy. Let them be reminders that God is your source, and that there are many channels and ways for God's good to flow into your life. When you are tempted to focus too much attention on what you don't have, make a conscious decision to shift your focus to what you already have, and decide to appreciate it and enjoy it more fully and completely. Think of all the simple things you take for granted and thank God for them. Realize that each simple joy in life is God whispering that you are loved and supported by an abundant universe.

The obvious is that which is never seen until someone expresses it simply.

—KAHLIL GIBRAN

Here are a few of the simple things in life, to remind you that you are already rich in the things that count. Let them inspire you to count your own joyful simplicities and become aware of how much good God brings into your life every day.

. . . hot potatoes, butter, salt, pepper

. . . water flowing freely from a tap

. . . clear skies after a storm

. . . a kiss and a hug

. . . a roof over your head

. . . a safe place to sleep at night

. . . walking shoes and a trail

. . . home cooking

. . . an unexpected compliment

. . . grandparents holding grandbabies

. . . a hot shower or bath

. . . toilets that flush, plumbing that works

. . . soap and water

Simplicity Is . . .

. . . a new book to read

. . . tea with your best friend

. . . a gentle wind in the tree tops

. . . the laughter of children

. . . dogs loving every second of life (and worshipping you no matter what you do)

. . . cats allowing you to be their servants (dogs have owners, cats have staff)

. . . a lighted candle

. . . rainbows

. . . a flat tire repaired

. . . fresh raspberries

. . . bedtime stories for little ones

. . . fresh veggies from the garden

. . . a full tank of gas

. . . good neighbors

. . . family reunions

. . . an umbrella on a rainy day

. . . cheering for your team

. . . anything young and innocent

. . . a mountain view

. . . sacred scriptures in your faith tradition

. . . a deer in the forest

. . . open windows

. . . a check in the mail

. . . clean laundry

. . . a quiet moment alone

. . . the sound of a voice you love to hear

. . . evening prayer

ESSENTIALS OF THE HEART

One should never be nervous about being asked to tackle anything.
One has all the power necessary to achieve everything within oneself.
It is only necessary to remember the power. If people are nervous,
it is because they forget their potentialities and remember only their limitations.

—FRANK LLOYD WRIGHT

Simple and easy are not the same thing. Simplicity brings ease, but it is not always easy. Easy is the wish for the magic bullet, an instant solution, or ten easy steps to perfection. Easy formulas that reduce life to quantifiable processes are the fascination of our times. But simplicity is more organic and complex, a pearl of great price that must be sought after with the heart, not just the head.

Easy is like having a crush on someone, with its high floating feelings that dissipate like morning mist when the heat of noonday arrives. But true simplicity draws from a consistent, committed love that lasts through all hours and challenges of the lengthening day.

Simplicity is the marriage of commitment and surrender, the ebb and flow of tides of change and growth, the long slow ripening of the fruit of the spirit.

It is learning a deeper, richer way of being present to life. In this simplicity we discover that we are greater than we know, wiser than we realize.

All this sounds quite wonderful and spiritual. But how does this play out in daily life? How do we bring simplicity down to earth after spinning airy pictures of what our lives could be? What does simplicity look like in your life?

Simplicity is found in the common objects and objectives of each day. It is in the choices to create inner stillness through meditation and prayer, clearing clutter in both inner and outer life, choosing positive rather than negative thoughts, handling money and resources wisely, and making that which is most meaningful to you a priority. Whether it is in clothing that expresses your style and values, or a home that provides a nurturing atmosphere, or meaningful work that satisfies your creative soul and helps others, or loving relationships that balance giving and receiving, or creating a more sustainable and just society, true simplicity integrates our gifts, talents, and choices with the deep needs of the world. Inner simplicity helps us find a way to become who we were meant to be, allowing us to discover the amazing person God created and to see that amazing creativity and potential in every person we encounter.

Simplicity makes space for the old fashioned virtues to flower in our lives. Like clearing the garden of weeds and pests, simplicity prepares the soil and tends it as the flower and fruit of our inner selves mature. It is a tending of the garden of the soul. As the fruit of the spirit—love, joy, peace, patience, kindness, goodness, faithfulness, gentleness, self control—grows within, it will affect your practical outer life as well. Choosing to order your priorities around spiritual truth leads to true freedom.

Simplicity that revolves around the essentials of the heart creates a more fulfilling life. Choosing simplicity helps you make room for the important things in life: love, friendship, beauty, fun, creativity, and following your heart to a place of deep wholeness and peace.

Simplicity is . . . living in the moment to make each moment count.

Whenever a mind is simple, it is able to receive divine wisdom; old things pass away; it lives now and absorbs past and future into the present hour.

—RALPH WALDO EMERSON

Anyone can carry his burden, however hard, until nightfall.
Anyone can do his work, however hard, for one day.
Anyone can live sweetly, patiently, lovingly, purely, till the sun goes down.
And this is all that life really means.

—ROBERT LOUIS STEVENSON

SPIRITUAL MAGNIFICENCE

I am an expression of life, and life will express itself through me in the most playful and wonderful ways, if I let it.

—RICHARD BACH

The art of simplicity is not about reducing yourself to a smaller size. It's about clearing the clutter and chaos to make room for your God-given inner greatness to grow and expand.

Every person is born with the potential for true greatness. This is not the greatness of fame or fortune, though those may come as a by-product of bringing your inner resources to fruition. No, this potential is like a quiet seed within, waiting to be cultivated so that it might grow and multiply and make its contribution to the world.

Think of the size of a seed: so small, so insignificant, so seemingly lifeless. A petunia seed is barely the size of a grain of sand, yet when you plant this seed in fertile soil, water and fertilize and tend it, keep the ground clear of invasive weeds and hungry pests, this seed will naturally and effortlessly create a living, growing, luxurious plant with spreading green leaves and glorious blossoms. All of this potential is hiding in the tiny seed, just waiting for the right conditions to release the powerful life force within.

You are just like that seed. You may feel tiny and insignificant in this world, but you contain within your very being the nature of this ever evolving and ever expanding universe. You are a Big Bang waiting to happen; a transforming life force wants to flow through you and become life-giving love, joy, peace, and plenitude. The source of true abundance lies within you, if you are willing to create the conditions for it to manifest through you.

You can create the conditions for such a spiritual and material flowering. It takes simple, practical choices to weed out that which no longer serves you to make room for the higher good to grow. You can also access the wisdom of others who have discovered secrets of abundance and joy. You have the potential to become more fully free and alive than you dared dream you could be. The power lies not in words and ideas, but in what you choose to do with them. For when you unleash the God-given gifts that sleep in the center of your very being, you will awaken to your own spiritual magnificence, and to the great good you are meant to create in a world that is waiting for the gifts you have to offer.

And you, in your heart of hearts, know this to be true. This little book affirms the truth that you've always suspected but have been afraid to believe. You knew it as a young child. And you can know it again as an adult. It is not the outer circumstances that dictate what you can become, but what you can become that will create circumstances you desire. If you are willing to do the work that will free the seed of life to grow within, then you can transform yourself, change your circumstances, and make a real difference in the world around you. You can learn to enjoy the life you have, and to create a life you enjoy.

Your doubting mind will always find reasons to disbelieve, but your inner heart knows the truth. Eye has not seen and ear has not heard what God has prepared for those who dare to believe—and who dare to do something simple, practical, and meaningful with that belief. That is the true art of simplicity: getting down to the essentials, clearing the way for God to do the work in and through you.

And we, who with unveiled faces all reflect the Lord's glory,
are being transformed into his likeness with ever-increasing glory,
which comes from the Lord, who is the Spirit.

—II CORINTHIANS 3:18 (NIV)

You are an evolving person. You have come out of all time and are going to all time,
from glory to glory, led by an image of the Lord.
There is a perfect image at the center to cause what you are.
We don't have to manufacture goodness . . . just let it through.

—RAYMOND CHARLES BARKER

Religion is realization;
not talk, nor doctrine, nor theories however beautiful they may be.
It is being and becoming, not hearing, or acknowledging;
it is the whole soul becoming what it believes.

—SWAMI VIVEKANANDA

We will discover the nature of our particular genius
when we stop trying to conform to our own or to other people's models,
learn to be ourselves, and allow our natural channel to open.

—SHAKTI GAWAIN

My business is not to remake myself,
But to make the absolute best of what God made.

—ROBERT BROWNING

I see life in terms of transformation:
matter being transformed into life, life into consciousness,
consciousness into Divine Experience.

—BEDE GRIFFITHS

It takes courage to grow up and turn out to be who you really are.

—E.E.CUMMINGS

To be what we are, and to become what we are capable of becoming,
is the only end in life.

—ROBERT LOUIS STEVENSON

Affirmative Prayer

I am deeply connected with the Infinite Mind that created the Universe. This Infinite Power is within me and I now choose to nurture the God-given gifts that wait like seeds within my heart. I dare to dream a larger dream for my life, because my dreams come from God and are the blueprints for a way for me to be a blessing to the world I live in. I have the power to create great abundance. I now claim that power, sense it growing and expanding within. I know that this power is the Life Force wishing to express itself through me. I welcome this living, loving energy into my life and know that I am being transformed in this moment. I choose to nurture this seed of faith within and to cultivate spiritual fruit in my life. Before I prayed, God has already answered, and I rejoice in the flow of energy, passion, goodness, and joy that overflows in my heart. I thank God that this is so.

And so it is.

Simplicity is . . . being willing to believe what you know deep in your heart.

Balance and Strength

In walking, just walk. In sitting, just sit.
Above all, don't wobble.

—YUN MEN

INTEGRITY AND WHOLENESS

At each man's birth there comes into being
an eternal vocation for him, expressly for him.
To be true to himself in relation to this eternal vocation
is the highest thing a man can practice.

—SØREN KIERKEGAARDE

The bedrock of inner simplicity is integrity, the true integration of who you are with how you live. By not being true to your deepest self, you end up living a lie, even when you sincerely mean it for the best. If you are trying to squeeze yourself into a mold of someone else's making, or what you think someone else wants you to be, you are not living in full integrity. Your motives may be sincere. But every step away from becoming the essential you leads to detours and delays. You may be born to express one gift, but you run away from your own greatness when you settle for some pre-conceived notion of who you should be and what you can do.

We all begin in life with certain interests and abilities. One person loves to draw horses and dreams of raising Arabian horses in the West. Another dreams of trucks and rolling down the highway in search of adventure. Another yearns for a cozy cottage and a white picket fence. Certain things bring us to life, making us feel we are in the center of the flow of life. But as we grow older we are often told to set those dreams and interests aside for something more "sensible." The horsewoman decides it would be safer to be a secretary. The adventurer ends up working in a warehouse.

The very places where we should be encouraged to live our dreams—family, school, church—become prisons of unmet expectations and frustrated yearnings. Even our faith traditions can weigh us down with dogma and disapproval if we do not fit the prescribed roles of the religious sub-culture we belong to. So a woman stifles a dream of being an entrepreneur, trying to be satisfied as a mom and a Sunday school teacher. Or a man sets aside his artistic ambition to be a businessman and an elder in the church, wondering why he doesn't find his life more fulfilling. All of these roles are wonderful and worthy, in and of themselves. But if they don't come from the heart, they will never satisfy the soul. Yet we, with the best of intentions, often assume that our deeper yearnings were mere dreams of a naïve childhood that must be set aside so we can meet the obligations and satisfy the expectations of the "adult" world.

It actually takes more energy to deny dreams and desires than it does to pursue them. For example, I have discovered that when I write to satisfy the agendas of others and limit myself to their ideas of what is acceptable and appropriate, my energy is low, the work drags, and I feel as if I'm carrying the weight of the world on my shoulders. But when I'm free to move beyond those limits and express who I really am, I feel more alert and alive. I am energized, ideas flow, and life feels like an adventure full of endless possibilities. Demanding and difficult assignments have helped me become a better writer, functioning like a boot camp to polish my skills. Yet no matter how worthy the project and noble the cause, if it doesn't reflect who I am inside, it just doesn't have the zest and momentum of work done for love.

Even with obstacles and setbacks, as I step out in spite of my fears to do what I love, it is as if an inner compass points the way through unknown territory, carrying me in a flow of unfolding circumstances that feel like invisible hands helping me along. That's what happens when I make choices with integrity, honoring my heart instead of living by my ego's agendas.

Each day brings another opportunity to live life from the heart. Simple choices help you make a gentle course correction, eventually changing the trajectory of your life. Saying "yes" to your heart and "thank you for sharing but I'm going to put my heart's agenda first" to your ego will help you grow gradually into a more satisfying way of life. You don't have to work out every detail of "how" life will be transformed into a more satisfying way of being, you just have to take each opportunity as it comes, making choices that reflect an inner integrity that trusts what you feel in your heart, allowing your feelings and intuition to act as compasses that point to true north.

You can explore new ideas and opportunities in the context of the life you already live. The frustrated entrepreneur doesn't have to stop being a mother and a Sunday school teacher, but she can choose to take a business class and start exploring small business opportunities. The adventure of a lifetime can begin when the warehouse worker decides to take a weekend jaunt down a country road. A woman who feels constrained by a religious subculture can explore church history, theology, and metaphysics to help her discern the difference between dogma and authentic faith. Riding lessons or a week at a dude ranch may satisfy the heart of the horse lover, even if Arabian horse ranches in the West are not her destiny.

Begin where you are and remember that the choices you have made, both good and bad, have helped you become the person you are. You did the best you could with what you knew at the time. Value that experience and use it as a springboard to make better, more empowering choices now. Trust that nothing is wasted and that God can work everything together for the highest good. Every day brings opportunities to choose something you want, to work toward a cherished dream, to explore a long-held interest. Small choices can change your life gently and gradually, without fanfare or uproar. The choices you made yesterday created the life you live today. The choices you make today create the life you will lead tomorrow. Choosing to align your choices with your deepest dreams and heart's desires will lead, sooner or later, to a life lived in integrity and wholeness.

Simplicity is . . . being true to yourself.
Simplicity is . . . thanking God that all things can work together for good.

Go to your bosom; knock there and ask your heart what it doth know.

—WILLIAM SHAKESPEARE

It's so hard to believe that what the world wants is us.
It's hard to believe, whatever you're doing, that you're enough.
We are all, always, enough.

—BARBARA COOK

You must speak straight so your words may go as sunlight to our hearts.

—COCHISE, CHIRICAHUA APACHE

Do not condemn the world.
Deify the world by your deeds, purify the world by your utterances,
and ennoble the world by your presence.

—SELVARAJAN YESUDIAN

Do not say a thing. What you are thunders so,
that I cannot hear what you say to the contrary.

—RALPH WALDO EMERSON

You can tell more about a monk by the way he uses his broom
than by anything he says.

—THOMAS MERTON

The most common form of despair is not being who you are.

—SØREN KIERKEGAARDE

He who would have beautiful roses in his garden
must have beautiful roses in his heart.

—DEAN SAMUEL HOLE

If your thought is a rose,
you will be the rose garden.

—RUMI

The place in the monastery which is closest to God is not the church,
but the garden. There the monks are at their happiest.

—SAINT PACHOMINA

The old plum tree withstands all conditions—
sometimes it faces spring, sometimes winter;
sometimes it faces strong wind, sometimes storms;
sometimes it is pure fragrance.

—ZEN MASTER DOGEN

Every person is given something to do
that shows who God is.

—I CORINTHIANS 12:7 (THE MESSAGE)

Go where the love is!

—BARRY DEAN

Let yourself be drawn by the stronger pull of what you really love.

—RUMI

GETTING GROUNDED: MOVING MEDITATION INTO THE BODY

By matter we are nourished, lifted up, linked to everything else, invaded by life.

—PIERRE TEILHARD DE CHARDIN

When Native American medicine men talk to the sick, they ask these questions:

- When was the last time you sang?
- When was the last time you danced?
- When was the last time you told your story?
- When was the last time you rested in silence?

We live in a competitive society that doesn't take song, movement, story, or silence very seriously, considering such things as "frills." If it's not "useful" to the bottom line, it's ignored. Even when song, dance, and story are important, we are encouraged to be an audience to professional storytellers, dancers, and musicians. In our admiration for the polished performances of others, we lose sight of the importance of our own experience. We need to enter into the physicality of movement and sound and drama, for it is the very ground of our being awakening us to the fullness of life, anchoring us to the intimate simplicities of earth and body. It also anchors us in the moment as we draw back into the body's experience of the here and now. The antidote to a civilization obsessed with brain power is to plunge into the body, diving deep into the pool of our own being.

If you wish to calm an agitated spirit, you need to ground yourself in the body. Your body is a God-given wonder that offers its own path to spiritual experience. You experience life with your body, so body-oriented prayer, meditation, movement, and communication can be a rich source of nourishment and comfort. One way to describe this entrance into earth and body is grounding. In Tai Chi, yoga, and belly dance, for instance, you are encouraged to imagine your feet rooting into the ground, just as a tree sends its tap roots deep into the soil to receive nourishment. Take off your shoes, get closer to the earth, and feel yourself become more connected to the ground beneath you. Take a deep breath, draw energy from the earth and then exhale and let your anxiety drain back into the receptive soil and rock. Joy Manné describes it in her book, *Conscious Breathing*. She says, "Grounding is initiatory. It increases the amount of energy we have available, focuses it, and brings us face to face with life. Being grounded means being in the present, in clear conscious contact with our physical body, thoughts, and non-physical energy field in such a way that we derive strength, stability, and information from all of them."

I have discovered the power of being grounded through drumming, dancing, healing touch, singing, and meditative movement like walking and belly dance. I attend a women's drumming circle that gathers—rain or shine, heat or cold—every month on the night of the full moon. We drum and dance, then share our stories. I joke a bit, calling us Campfire Goddesses or Goddess Scouts, for it reminds me of the outdoor fire circles I enjoyed as a girl at summer camp. We come from many backgrounds and beliefs; we are many ages and at different stages in our lives. Yet as we sit in the great outdoors and pass the talking stick around the circle, each woman's story is a reflection of my story. We are sisters who live in closer harmony with the energies of the earth, bringing that time of grounding back into our daily lives.

I discovered the grounding power of belly dance, an ancient Middle Eastern dance form for a woman to move her body in celebration. The movements of belly dance help strengthen a woman for the process of birth, building the abdominal muscles and bringing greater flexibility to the spine. The sensuous spiral movements of the dance enchant me. I also adore the colorful "girlie" jingle belts, sparkles and spangles, silken veils, and creative costumes. Look up "belly dance" on the Internet and you'll see that there's a whole wonderful world of creativity and beauty available, a growing subculture of women who are discovering the joy of inner power by moving their bodies in a feminine way. When I do a few simple hip circles, figure eights, or undulations to a soothing rhythm, I calm down, feel more relaxed, and enter into a softer, gentler frame of mind. I also sleep better and have more energy after dance class.

I also ground myself with walks in nature. I love to go to a nearby lake and walk the trails. A doe and her fawn may cross my path, and I see in her eyes a reflection of my own wild life. Cicadas sing in the summer, surrounding me with a sensory vibration of sound. Winter brings winds and cool sun shining through the bare branches; spring the rushing sounds of full creeks; fall the crunch of crisp leaves beneath my feet. An hour's walk at the lake replenishes my spirit and renews my mind.

You can ground yourself with moving meditation and being in nature. It will help you cope with—and transcend—a modern life of machines, artificial light, controlled environments, traffic, and deadlines. Turn off the computer, put the cell phone on hold, and walk away from the "to do" list to take time for just "being."

Here are some simple ways to get grounded:

- ❖ Take a deep breath. Now let it out with a sigh. Ahhhh. Deep breathing does wonders for relaxing the body, clearing the mind, and releasing tension.
- ❖ Sing—alone or with others. Your voice is an instrument that will tune body and soul.
- ❖ Take a walk in nature. Whether it is a city park, a waterside path, a country road, or a wild tangled forest, Mother Nature embraces you and nurtures you when you go outside to be with her.
- ❖ Dig in a garden. From modest planters on an apartment deck to suburban flowerbeds to spreading acres of fruit orchards and vegetable gardens, digging in the dirt and nurturing plants will help you weed out old thoughts and make room for the seeds of new ideas and fresh perspectives.
- ❖ Take a dance or movement class. I love belly dance, but there are many forms of moving meditation and exercise available, including yoga, Tai Chi, and Nia dance, which is a combination of many movement forms that draws from tae kwon do, jazz dance, yoga, modern dance, and other fitness forms. Or consider group dancing: folk, contra, circle, swing, salsa—you name it, you can find a class that will show you how to dance it.

- Explore the fun of drums, rattles, and other rhythm instruments. There are many drum circles available where people join to drum, dance, and have a good time. Rhythm entrains your body, helping you to relax and enter into higher states of consciousness. I am always amazed at how much clarity I feel after spending a couple of hours drumming with a group.
- A nap can be grounding, helping you to release your cares and wake up with a better perspective on life.
- Interplay is a wonderful form of body movement and group interaction that creates opportunities for community as well as personal healing. Interplay takes the best from art, liturgy, and therapy to playfully reintegrate body and spirit. I have thoroughly enjoyed all my experiences with Interplay. Check out their web site at interplay.org for more information.

Our own physical body possesses a wisdom that we who inhabit the body lack.

—HENRY MILLER

The glory of God is a fully alive person.

—IRANEUS

Being grounded is empowering. Once we are grounded and in tune with the earth's energy, we are also in tune with a higher energy that is above the earth. This energy is traditionally called Heaven in symbolic language. Symbolically, as we walk upright, we connect to heaven and earth.

—JOY MANNÉ

Meditation has nothing to do with quiet reverie or passive stillness, but with wakefulness. We awaken our nearness to God. We realize that the power of creation, the energy of creation, flows in our hearts.

—JOHN MAIN

This is yoga rhythm—the unifying pulse. Like the current of a river, this pulse is sometimes strong, invigorating and vibrant while at other times tranquil, serene, and effortless. Each variation is sacred, from the dynamic to the meditative.

—SHIVA REA

With an eye made quiet by the power of harmony and the deep power of joy, we see into the life of things.

—WILLIAM WORDSWORTH

Live so that you are at ease, in harmony
with the world, and full of joy.
Day and night, share the springtime with all things,
thus creating the seasons in your own heart.
This is called achieving full harmony.

—CHUANG TSU

As a result of my work, I can no longer consider the body as organic systems of tissues. The healthy body is a flowing, interactive electrodynamic energy field. Motion is more natural to life than non-motion—things that keep flowing are inherently good. What interferes with flow will have detrimental effects.

—VALERIE HUNT

Nothing is more revealing than movement.

—MARTHA GRAHAM

Nothing happens till something moves.

—ALBERT EINSTEIN

DANCE WITH LIFE TO REFRESH YOUR SPIRIT

"Whosoever knows the power of dance dwells in God."

—RUMI

Are you in a creative slump? Do you feel like you're in a rut? Would you like to add more zest to your life? Think about moving your body and relaxing your mind. If you're feeling stressed, burned out, or tied up in knots, tapping into the wisdom of the body can move you out of a creative dead end into the flow of renewal and refreshment.

Moving the body is medicine for the soul. We were created to sing, dance, play, clap our hands, and express ourselves with our entire being. Yet our society has taught us to lock ourselves into rigid mental boxes, treating our bodies as mere containers for the self-important brain. We are told that it's okay for children to play, but that being an adult is serious business. We are also taught to look at our bodies as meat machines with a computer brain running the show instead of seeing ourselves as an organic whole: body, mind, soul, and spirit in a constant dialogue.

Like the tight corsets and stiff collars of yesteryear, we need to let go of old images and beliefs which no longer serve us. Yet we often live as if we were still encased in constraining clothing, unable to move freely—in fact we don't begin to realize how free we could be. Rhythm and movement can help us move out of the constraints of our mental corsets into the flowing freedom of the body. The body experiences life as an integrated whole, a world of sensation and intuition and movement that relaxes us into a wider and fuller understanding of our place in the universe.

"Our world has changed.
Accessing our body wisdom is more vital than ever.
We are taking in enormous amounts of information every day.
We need ways to move heaviness out of our bodies,
create clear space, pray,
and stay in touch with our deepest purpose.
Most importantly we need
simple things like: breath, the touch of a hand,
stillness, dance, stories, and songs."

—CYNTHIA WINTON-HENRY, CO-FOUNDER/CREATOR OF INTERPLAY

I have rediscovered the joy of moving my body with childlike freedom. As a writer, I often live life in my head. Creating a secondhand experience of life on the page, I forget to go out and experience life itself. I was going through a stressful transition when I sought new ways to move beyond the limitations of my situation and viewpoint. I decided that it was time to try something new that would introduce me to fresh ideas and experiences. Drumming and dancing fit the bill.

I attended my first drum circle on a January night at a retreat center just outside of Nashville. A friend sponsored it and gathered over fifty friends to celebrate with her. It was cold outside and the stars seemed to be frozen in the sky. But inside the lodge there was warmth and light and laughter. The room was full of energy as people clapped and drummed and danced. It was a magical evening.

The drum circle facilitator divided us into groups and taught us different rhythms, showing us how to listen to one another in the call and answer of the drum beat. We were encouraged to combine rhythms in creative ways. The direction was so easy and encouraging that even the shyest people warmed to the rhythm and began to keep time in harmony with the group. I felt the same kind of liberty I had known as a child; a sense of fun, freedom, and creativity that provided a release from the stress of my day. There were smiles all around the circle. And everyone, from the most expert drummer to the newbie shaking a rattle or clapping hands, was included. No one was left out. Everyone was welcome to participate in whatever way that was comfortable for them.

A few months later, the drum facilitator, Ed Haggard, offered beginning drum lessons. Since I had been attracted to the drums for a long time, I decided it was time to get some rhythm going in my life. So I went to Ed's class and discovered the beautiful sounds of the *djembe*, a goblet-shaped drum made in one piece from a hollowed out tree trunk, covered with a shaved goatskin. The *djembe* is known in many parts of Africa and has been used for centuries to call the community together, celebrate the ancient stories, and communicate the traditions and beliefs of the village family. This drum is played with the hands and offers many tonal variations, depending on how and where you strike the skin. It is a rich and beautiful instrument, resonant when held by the body. The *djembe* has been called the healing drum and heal it does. As I have played in the group, my heart (which is also a natural drum) has been healed and comforted.

Working with a wonderful leader and teacher, the class is a safe place for everyone to try a new skill. Ed describes drumming as dancing with your hands. He helps the group find its rhythm together. In the beginning I felt like I had two left hands, but by the end of the first lesson I had developed enough confidence to drum away like a happy child. I had tasted drum magic and was hooked. I went home feeling energized and optimistic.

Now I own a handmade *djembe*, with a hand carved wooden shell from Africa. I chose the goatskin to cover the shell, plus the ropes and fabric to finish it. Ed made it for me and created a beautiful heart shape on the skin head when he shaved the goatskin. It is a gorgeous instrument, deeply satisfying to play.

Drumming with the group is a great tension reliever. I can feel the drum energy right down to my bones. When I'm stressed out at home, worrying about some problem, I can set my worries aside and create a meditative moment by banging away on my *djembe* or on mini bongos or by shaking a rattle. Satisfying rhythm can be created anywhere on anything that the hand can tap, slap, or strike. Repetition and rhythm create a more meditative flow as my mind drifts with the music of the beat. If I'm frustrated or angry, drumming offers a good outlet for my feelings, calming me and helping me regain my perspective.

The delights of self-discovery are always available.

—GAIL SHEEHY

Drum class led me to my next adventure in movement: belly dancing. I decided to give it a try. I soon learned that a good belly dancer is a good athlete. She's flexible and is able to move different parts of her body in different rhythms—and be graceful at the same time! Belly dancing teaches a woman to know her body in new ways. If I felt like I had two left hands in my first drum class, I discovered that I had a dozen uncoordinated body parts in my first belly dance class. Even so, by the end of class I was picking up some basic moves. And what a workout! Even more wonderful was the way I felt the next day. I was energized, alert, and able to move calmly through the stresses of the work day. I was also a little sore, but that soon went away. What didn't go away was how good I felt. Each class since has helped me not only build skill, but strength, flexibility, and stamina. The energy is amazing. I am definitely hooked on belly dancing.

Belly dancing, also known as Middle Eastern dance, is all about flexibility and femininity. In her book, *Grandmother's Secrets: The Ancient Rituals and Healing Power of Belly Dancing*, author Rosina-Fawzin Al-Rawa says, "One might object that belly dancing originates in a culture which is foreign to the West and therefore unsuited to Western women, yet this is precisely what makes it an even more enriching experience, apart from the fact that it is perfectly suited to the female body . . . New worlds of awareness become accessible, releasing memories stored in the body and a joyful physicality that leads to a less rigid way of life."

"The human body is a wondrous thing."

—RALPH STRAUCH

Drums and dance cross cultural boundaries and speak to us without words. Music therapy studies show that rhythm directly affects the psyche. Changes in muscle tone, breath, and oxygen in the blood have been measured medically in both those who play and those who hear the rhythm. These simple activities release the inner healing power of our bodies.

Rhythm cultures of the world have learned that drumming and moving the body brings people together in harmony and equality. Percussionist Mickey Hart says, "The drum is blind to gender, race, or how much money you make per year. It is a perfect lesson in equality. In a drum group, everybody is a winner who participates with an open heart and mind." Whether you play a drum, dance to the beat, clap your hands, or sing along, you can participate. Everyone contributes to the circle of sound and sensation. Express the delight of being alive, the joy of movement, the magic of sound. Live fully and deeply in the here and now. Connect to the simple wisdom of your body. Join the circle of smiling faces. There's always room for one more!

The roots of both depth psychology and dance therapy can be traced to earliest human history, when disease was seen as a loss of soul and dance was an intrinsic part of the healing ritual.

—PATRIZIA PALLERO

Dancers are the athletes of God.

—ALBERT EINSTEIN

An old woman is never old when it comes to the dance she knows.

—IBO PROVERB

Heaven is under our feet as well as over our heads.

—HENRY DAVID THOREAU

The earth braces itself for the feet of a lover of God about to dance.

—HAFIZ

To watch us dance is to hear our hearts speak.

—HOPI SAYING

I dance for myself and for the city.

—ZUNI INDIAN SAYING

I have heard that the body listens to rhythms the mind can't even hear.
The wind and the sunset are like a dog whistle to the bones,
but the mind is deaf to their high, clear missive.

—JOHN LEE

The sun shines not on us, but in us. The rivers flow not past, but through us, thrilling, tingling, vibrating every fiber and cell of the substance of our bodies, making them glide and sing.

—JOHN MUIR

Think like a river.
Sing like a mountain.

—MARY DE LA VALETTE

Those who don't feel this life pulling them like a river, those who don't drink dawn like a cup of springwater or take in a sunset like supper, those who don't want to change, let them sleep.

—RUMI

The world speaks to me in colors, my soul answers in music.

—RABINDRANATH TAGORE

Earth with her thousand voices praises God.

—SAMUEL TAYLOR COLERIDGE

I tell you, if these were silent, the very stones would cry out.

—JESUS

LUKE 19:40 (RSV)

The song and the land are one.

—BRUCE CHATWIN

Meaning seems to leap out of matter, like a tiger out of a dark cave.

—RAMAKRISHNA

There are unknown forces in nature;
when we give ourselves wholly to her, without reserve, she leads them to us;
she shows us those forms which our watching eyes do not see,
which our intelligence does not understand or suspect.

—AUGUSTE RODIN

Believe us who have experience, you will find more
laboring amongst woods than ever you will amongst books.
Woods and stones will teach you more than any master.

—BERNARD OF CLAIRVAUX

For you shall go out in joy;
and be led forth in peace;
the mountains and the hills before you
shall break forth into singing,
and all the trees of the field
shall clap their hands.

—ISAIAH 55:12 (RSV)

SURRENDER YOUR RESISTANCE: POWER *VS.* FORCE

Flow is being aligned with that which propels our lives.

—JUDITH ORLOFF

In the movie *Out of Africa* there is a creek that is dammed when Karen Blixen builds her coffee farm. By the end of the movie, and at the end of her time in Africa, the river floods, the dam breaks, and the waters can no longer be held back. She opens her hands, releasing the water, and the farm she fought so hard to keep. She says to the natives helping her, "This water is for Mombasa. Let it go. Let it go."

How often I have tried to control and confine my life, living according to old rules, ideas, and expectations. I've wasted so much energy on proving I was right, on resisting change, and on trying to hold onto the past long after it was time to let it go. It took me a long time to become conscious that another way was possible—a more flexible and easy way to approach life. I have learned that there is great power in living in the flow.

Like a river, the life force must find its own way. There is something deep within that urges us to grow and evolve, to expand and to move beyond the limits of the way we were. We grow and evolve through different stages of life. Though a mother may adore the cuddly child, the nature of childhood is growth, expansion, and movement toward adulthood. It would be unnatural to try to stop the child from growing into an adult. As adults, we, too, are always going through stages of growth and change. Time moves on even when we wish it would stand still. The wisest course of action is to savor the moment and then release it, trusting that the next moment will bring its own gifts into our lives.

Your work really begins when you release the struggle.
To let go of struggle initiates a change of vibration within you.
This change puts you in touch with the flow of Life Itself,
which is essentially what you are.
To cultivate your awareness of this flow is your real work.

—SWAMI CHETANANANDA

Proceed as the way opens.

—QUAKER PROVERB

Sometimes we try to force things to happen. Yet our anxiety and urgency block the very flow we desire. The ego loves to control, confine, define. But the freedom of the spirit moves according to a deeper wisdom. Jesus told Nicodemus, "The wind blows wherever it pleases. You hear its sound, but you cannot tell where it comes from or where it is going. So it is with everyone born of the Spirit." (John 3:8 NIV) Life lived from a more spiritual perspective must enter into the flow of creation and allow Divine Timing to bring the desired results into our lives.

Flowing with life is not merely a passive allowing, but a co-creative act with God. You do your best, but then leave the rest up to God. Just as a farmer prepares the soil, plants the seeds, waters and cultivates the land, and does his daily work, so you do what you can do to create the optimum conditions for what you desire. It is the life force within the seed and the seed's partnership with the elements that create the magic of growth and fruition. The farmer does not have to stand in the field, grunting and groaning, trying to make the seeds grow. He plants the seed and trusts its nature to fulfill its destiny. You, too, can plant and cultivate your seeds of faith and watch them grow according to a greater wisdom than you can yet imagine.

When you tap into the greater Life Force, acknowledging God as your true source, something opens up, releases, and moves with greater ease and flexibility. The more you resist, the harder life is. If you are willing to be flexible and open, you'll discover a gentle strength greater than you could have imagined in your earlier power struggles. Surrender your resistance. Go with the flow. And let it lead you into more fulfilling adventures.

Simplicity is . . . letting go and letting God.

Like water, the sage should wait
for the moment to ripen and be right.
Water, you know, never fights.
It flows around
without harm.

—TAO TE CHING

You can't push a wave onto the shore
any faster than the ocean brings it in.

—SUSAN STRASBERG

If it don't fit, don't force it.

—ROY CLARK

Just trust yourself, then you will know how to live.

—GOETHE

You are so weak. Give up to grace.
The ocean takes care of each wave
till it gets to shore.
You need more help than you know.

—RUMI

The way to do is to be.

—LAO TZU

If we could just be,
we would be able to relax from the anxiety of becoming something we are not,
getting something we don't have,
and trying to shape reality according to our own desires.

—KABIR EDMUND HELMINSKI

Anyone who holds on to life just as it is destroys that life.
But if you let it go, reckless in your love,
you'll have it forever, real and eternal.

—JOHN 12:25 (THE MESSAGE)

Light will someday split you open
even if your life is now a cage,
for a divine seed, the crown of destiny
is hidden and sown on an ancient
and fertile plain you hold title to.

—HAFIZ

Simple things, simple fun, simply living:

. . . funky international restaurants serving delicious exotic dishes

. . . a catlike stretch releasing and relaxing the muscles

. . . a church full of people singing the grand old hymns

. . . fresh basil and homegrown tomatoes

. . . the feel of sand between your toes

. . . the mathematical elegance of Baroque music

. . . reading seed catalogs and planning the perfect garden in January

. . . a parking place in a busy city

. . . lullabies in the night

. . . a beautiful woman who doesn't know how beautiful she is

. . . an unselfconscious child

. . . wild creatures going about their daily business

. . . cicadas singing an end of summer song

. . . crafts for sale at a crafts fair

. . . a string of pearls

. . . a mother cat with a basketful of nursing kittens

. . . the "regulars" at their favorite watering hole

. . . fund raisers for a good cause

. . . moving your body simply for the joy of moving

. . . hands on a drum creating a healing rhythm to dance to

. . . a delicious new dish you've never tasted before

. . . festivals that celebrate world cultures

. . . subways and skyscrapers in the big city

. . . baseball on a sunny spring day

. . . vanilla ice cream and hot chocolate sauce

. . . keeping a promise

. . . fan clubs and autograph lines

. . . a road that takes you where you want to go

. . . taking the high road

Managing Your Resources

All our acts have sacramental possibilities.

—FREYA STARK

CLEARING CLUTTER: RELEASING THAT WHICH NO LONGER SERVES

The Law of Circulation works at many levels—the emotional and mental as well as the material. Wherever you release the old and remove that which blocks the flow of spiritual energy, you increase the flow of good.

—DAVID OWEN RITZ

When most people think of simplicity, they think of clean closets and empty spaces, organized lives and cleared schedules. While simplicity does manifest in those forms, inner simplicity does not depend on outward circumstances. When you clear the clutter within, you'll eventually see a corresponding outer simplicity. But if you are full of chaos within, even a simple life will become littered with unfinished business and unnecessary drama. Choosing to cultivate inner simplicity helps you develop a mature way of life that has its own focus and order, even if your daily life is busy and complex.

One of the most difficult things to do is to release things, ideas, and relationships that no longer serve us. We often save every old thing, "just in case." You'll open a kitchen drawer and it will be filled with clutter: old rubber bands, pieces of string, used aluminum foil, and other miscellaneous bits and pieces. That kitchen drawer is a metaphor for life. Filled with things that you keep holding onto, pretty soon the drawer is so full you can't find anything at all. Even if you could remember what you've squirreled away in that drawer, you couldn't find it to use it. So you keep the drawer closed and start filling other drawers with more stuff you can't use and don't need any more.

We do that with our lives, too. Old grudges, old resentments, old attitudes, and old ways of coping—we'll keep them around because we've gotten used to them and aren't sure we'd know what to do without them. We'll stuff an old belief system that no longer works for us into a back drawer of our minds. Because it's still in there, it will affect our choices even when we're not conscious of it. For example, you might be meeting someone new who would be labeled in the old belief system as "unacceptable" and while you might now understand that every single person is beloved and beautiful, there will be a whisper of "unacceptable" even when you are trying your best to be open and friendly. Or you'll be looking in the mirror and suddenly it won't be the adult you're seeing, but the unhappy junior high student who felt ugly and didn't fit in. You are still carrying that old image of yourself, even though it is useless baggage that you could live without.

Old judgements, old priorities, old belief systems, old ways of doing things are all clutter that needs to be taken out and examined. If it still works for you, keep it. But if it's no longer helpful or distracts you from what is most important, maybe it's time to let it go. Some ideas and things are like timeless classics. They wear well, they're well made, and they still look good and are useful years later. Others are like clothing that is out of date and which no longer fits who you are now. It's time to let it all go and make room for something that is more aligned with who you are becoming.

It's time to choose voluntary simplicity. Paradoxically, sometimes arranging things and clearing space in your outer life can help you in the process of creating inner simplicity. The very act of sorting material things can help you sort your thoughts and priorities. Begin by releasing the things that you can no longer care for and attend to. Start with material things—cleaning closets, attics, basements, storerooms, and garages. Give away or sell what could be useful to others. Put back into circulation those things which you've been holding onto. Organize what you decide to keep so you know where everything is and what is available to you.

Then take a look at your past and see what attitudes and beliefs no longer work for you. If you've been holding grudges against others, release them. If you've been hanging onto old regrets, let go and let God take care of the past. Long-standing judgments of others and of yourself no longer serve you. Wipe the slate clean and allow God to write a new story of hope and joy where the old one of hurt and anger used to be. Limited ideas and false beliefs keep you from exploring new ideas and widening your horizons. Let go of them, just as you let go of the old clothing you gave away. Let the healing energy of forgiveness release the limitations of resentment and destructive energy from your consciousness.

As you release the old, you'll make room for the good that God wants to bring into your life. You'll discover a new energy and zest, because you won't be using all your energy to carry around the old baggage. Clearing the clutter allows the energy to flow more freely, and you'll bring more focus and clarity to the way you live your life.

Simplicity is . . . releasing that which no longer serves me.

The depth of one's letting go determines the
depth of one's freedom.

—KAREN GOLDMAN

If you stop asking for what you do not need,
what you need will come to you.

—NISARGADATTA MAHARAJ

If one is afraid of losing anything, they have forgotten God's promise.

—HAFIZ

Dance with both arms free.

—RAMAKRISHNA

Taking a new step, uttering a new word,
is what people fear most.

—FYODOR DOSTOEVSKY

He who would create the new must be able to
endure the passing of the old in full tranquility.

—RUDOLF STEINER

Don't worry about mistakes.
Making things out of mistakes, that's creativity.

—PETER MAX

Imagination can't just be about reruns.
It also has to be about writing our own new script.

—THOMAS L. FRIEDMAN

Live out of your imagination, not your past.

—STEPHEN COVEY

HANDLING MONEY: CREATING PROSPERITY

Oh Man!
There is no planet, sun, or star could hold you,
if you but knew what you are.

—RALPH WALDO EMERSON

The Art of Simplicity would be incomplete without a chapter on money. Unresolved money issues can clutter your consciousness, making it difficult to think and act clearly. Facing the money dragon can free you from the chains of the past and empower you to create the life you've dreamed of instead of repeating familiar nightmares.

This is the chapter I would have liked to skip. Money has been, quite frankly, a big issue for me. And it has been an issue for much longer than I had hoped or anticipated. There are many questions of shame, self-worth, and trust tied up in money, and my feelings about having money and not having money have been more complicated than I wanted to admit, even to myself. I can't say that I've been a stellar example of prosperity consciousness through the years (quite the opposite), but when I decided to try a different way of looking at money, self-worth, and prosperity, I did begin to see the unhealthy patterns that had created most of my unhappy experiences with (and without) money. And I began to create a new experience with money that reflected a healthier understanding of who I am and what God wants to do in my life.

When I began my career as an author, visions of royalties and advances danced like sugarplums in my dreams. The act of writing a book is a statement of abundance, especially when your first book is titled, *The Art of Abundance*. And I enjoyed abundance. But there were issues of money and self-worth, and many changes in my career and in the publishing industry meant that the early promise of an easy upward trend turned into the ups and downs most authors are all too familiar with. One of my books was caught in a publisher bankruptcy, others didn't sell as well as expected, and staff changes and merger/buyouts meant that eventually my Art of books were no longer in print. One day that would change and I would find a delightful new publisher for these books, but there were many transitions to go through before that would happen.

Changes happened in my life, too, and though there was the thrill of a big royalty check and the hope for more books to be published, doors began to close, and opportunities melted away. No matter how hard I knocked, most doors seemed to stay tightly shut. As time went by, debts piled up and I existed in survival mode. Living week to week, watching the economy take a nosedive (especially difficult as freelance work dried up), mourning with the rest of the nation the unthinkable losses of 9/11, and seeing the death of so many dreams, it was a dark night of the soul for me. It was also a mirror that showed me the shadows I had been unwilling to look at until then.

I looked at questions of character and what I had done to contribute to the problem. I had to face my habits of feeding angry and fearful thoughts in my life. I needed to address those issues and learn to replace anger with love, fear with faith. I also needed to learn more about handling money. I mourned my losses, let the old dreams die, and asked myself, "What do I really believe?" "What do I truly desire?" "Who am I and why am I here?" Familiar questions were asked with a new urgency.

My questions were the beginning of a new way of being in the world, leading to the decision to let go of an old belief system that no longer worked for me, and to try new options. I didn't have answers at first, but even the simple act of asking questions was empowering for me. Did I really believe what I had been taught about God? Did I truly believe I deserved to struggle and be in debt? Was I necessarily doomed to failure, or was it a result not of capricious fate, but of my own choices made unconsciously and patterns perpetuated in ignorance? Did I have more power to change my life than I gave myself credit for? Was my God truly the Great Creator of abundance, and if so, why wasn't my life reflecting that abundance? What did I believe about my self-worth? about money? about success? What did I say I believed and how did my actions reflect that belief? Did I say I believed in a God of love and abundance, then make choices out of anger and fear? Did I believe that the Universe was a friendly place? Did I believe all those wise words I wrote about in my books? Was I willing to open my mind to new ideas and to allow God to expand my boundaries and move me beyond my comfort zone?

Raised by parents who lived through the Depression and World War II, money was often thought of in terms of scarcity, though generous giving was still the way they chose to live. We might be knee-deep in a river of abundance, but life was still colored by fears of scarcity. And when I was growing up in the United States at the end of the twentieth century, though abundance was all around us, the advertisements in the media always told us that we didn't have enough unless we purchased the product that was being pitched. If you didn't buy the hair lightener, you couldn't have the enviable life of the smiling blonde on the surfboard. If you bought the outfit, the skin cream, the hot car, the trip to Hawaii, it proved that you were "with it" and one of the chosen.

Only a few "special" people had that charisma, but you could buy it in a bottle or box.

Looking back, I realized I had bought into that mentality. I truly believed I was not enough, never could be or get enough, and that if I didn't have the right dress, hair color, car, or shoes, I wouldn't measure up to the standards set by all of the beautiful people. On top of that, my religion had an unspoken message that I was a sinner and deserved to struggle—or that somehow struggling made me more "spiritual" and that there was virtue in being poor. There was a lot of talk about grace, but almost everyone lived under the law. There were unconscious assumptions that if I didn't have the money to buy the right product, or if my life didn't look like the pictures in the magazines, then I must be a failure, a loser, a person who was born to struggle against unkind fate. I could turn my "failure" into a form of spiritual martyrdom, but in the end I was still a failure in the eyes of world. Even the religious people who thought that money was not supposed to be important gravitated toward those who looked more like the world's definition of success. You could talk about giving it all up for God, but the preachers and teachers and media stars seemed to have no problem with having plenty of the good things of life.

I had been wrestling with my beliefs for several years, trying to reconcile a theology that condemned my "unsaved" friends to hell with what I knew of them as precious and sacred people loved by God (even if they didn't believe in God as I understood God). This theology also talked about a generous God, but it was extremely cheap when it came to honoring those who served him. I saw a lot of penny pinching with businesses and ministries when it came to paying people what they were worth.

I had to come to terms with my own belief system. I was giving the same lip service as they to an abundant and loving God, but my thoughts were dark and pinched. I could see God in the abundance of nature, in the beautiful variety of faces of the people I loved, and in the small things of life that were not tied to money, prestige, or power. But my limited view of God didn't allow him to be involved too closely with "filthy lucre." The Bible verse says that the *love* of money is the root of all evil. But I was acting as if money itself was evil.

I had to examine my core beliefs. I also had to look at my attitudes. I might seem to be sweetness and light on the surface, but if there was darkness in my heart, it would surface in my thoughts and words and deeds. I began to realize that I was sowing seeds of doubt as well as debt when I whined, complained, blamed others, and allowed my decisions about money, career, and other life matters to be made from an attitude of fear instead of true faith. I was no better than the good-hearted people who mistakenly served a God of scarcity, anger, and judgment. I myself had created an idol of scarcity, anger, and judgment in my mind. I had to see that my problems stemmed from roots of fear, anger, and judgment within myself. Others may have taught me to view life that way, but I was the one who chose to buy into such a bankrupt belief system. I realized I had to look elsewhere to find the Source of my abundance.

Looking back now, I see that hitting bottom was a gift. I was so stubbornly holding onto my understanding of how things worked that I had worked my way into a hole. They say the only way to stop going deeper into the hole is to stop digging. After digging myself nearly to China, it was time to throw the shovel down and look for another way. And so, one baby step at a time, I began to make new choices.

I began to reinvent my life. I changed belief systems by being open to new ways of thinking, taking risks and trying new things. I didn't throw the Christ Child out with the bath water, but I did expand my understanding of religion, spirituality, faith, Christ, and God. I started reframing my experiences, stopped labeling myself a failure, and began to tell myself a new story about who I was and what kind of God I was connected to.

It didn't come all at once. It was a gradual change, one small step, one new idea at a time. These steps took me to a church where a more positive view of God and the meaning of our life here on earth is taught. I took up African drumming and belly dancing and met new friends who are committed to a more positive, open, and proactive view of life. Letting go of the old, which no longer served me, I began reading books that challenged old beliefs and brought me understanding from a fresh perspective. I made different decisions about where, how, when, and why I spent money. I continued creating new projects, yet I was more willing to wait till the timing was right instead of trying to force things to go the way I thought they should go. Being grateful for what I already had was key to my turnaround—whining was definitely out. Choosing to release anger, fear, judgement, and self pity helped me become clear on what I truly desired instead of constantly trying to be what I thought others wanted me to be.

I am still learning. It took years to create a mountain of debt and build bad habits into my life. It can take some time to unlearn old habits and embrace new ways and pay off debts. The voice of doubt can keep coming up. Consequences of past choices have to be dealt with, even if I am making new, more empowering choices. I have to untangle many beliefs and examine them, sorting out what is authentic spirituality and what is b.s. (belief system).

I have made tremendous progress, and I am reaching many of my goals—and aiming for greater goals than I was able to imagine before I made these new, empowering choices. That doesn't mean there aren't still struggles with money, self-worth, my understanding of God and how the universe works. Yet I see that the struggle is less about whether I have money or don't have money, and more about what I believe is possible, who I believe I am, and what kind of God I believe in. I've learned that you can have a scarcity mentality when you have a lot of money, and you can have a mentality of abundance even when you don't have much money. In the end, true prosperity lies in learning that God is my source. And my active faith allows God to fill my life with all the abundance, prosperity, and happiness I am willing to receive. As I expand my consciousness, I am empowered to manifest greater abundance in my life.

When doubts come, I choose to declare God as my Source, not money or the opinions of others, or even my own opinion of myself. On a frustrating day, when clients delay payment, and the mailbox is full of bills and advertisements, I can choose to trust in God as my source in spite of outward appearances. On a day when an anticipated check arrives or a long-term project finally bears financial fruit, I will still choose to trust God as my source. When I make choices that honor God, then I discover my spiritual magnificence.

I offer here a few of the insights I've discovered on this journey toward solvency and prosperity. I have used many of them to make progress and build success in my personal life, my financial situation, and my career track. I continue to learn new ways to apply them, and each time I open to a new idea or master a new skill, I see my life change for the better. I know that applying these principles can help you begin to change old patterns and make the choices that can transform your relationship with money, with God, and with yourself.

Life is ten percent what you make it,
and ninety percent how you take it.
—IRVING BERLIN

Your living is determined not so much by what life brings to you . . .
as by the attitude you bring to life.
—JOHN HOMER MILLS

You're blessed when you get your inside world—your mind and heart—put right. Then you can see God in the outside world.

—MATTHEW 5:8 (THE MESSAGE)

Any fact facing us is not as important as our attitude toward it, for that determines our success or failure.

—NORMAN VINCENT PEALE

MANIFESTING ABUNDANCE

If a person gets his attitude toward money straight,
it will help straighten out almost every other area in his life.

—BILLY GRAHAM

Our relationship with money reflects our attitudes about who we believe we are, what we believe we deserve, and the kind of God we serve. Money matters are deeply linked to spiritual matters. Money, especially in the United States at the dawn of the twenty-first century, is tied to our opinions of our own self-worth, and to our belief systems about God, abundance, scarcity, and how the universe works.

Paul wrote in Timothy 6:10, "For the love of money is a root of all kinds of evil." This verse has often been misquoted as "money is the root of all evil." But it is the *love* of money that is the root of many kinds of evil. This love of money is a form of idolatry, worshipping a false god. It is not limited to those who have money, for it is often those who do not have money who worship it the most. They believe that money will solve all their problems and make them whole, perfect, and complete. But anyone who has money will tell you that having a great deal of money creates its own set of problems. If you're unhappy, money will only allow you to be unhappy in nicer places. Unless you have a right relationship with money, it will create problems—or should I say, it will make you aware of the disconnect between what you claim to believe and what you truly believe about yourself.

There is a Power greater than earthly power, money, or material wealth. This inner Power is linked to a greater reality and true wealth. By choosing to connect to this Higher Power, you can become aligned in right relationship with money, creating a kind of abundance that is the Kingdom of Heaven manifested in and on earth. Whether you call that higher power God, Spirit, Buddha-nature, Christ-consciousness, the Inner Light, life force, good orderly direction, or quantum reality does not matter as much as that you are willing to open your heart to receive what you need: guidance, help, wisdom, and the material resources to create a life on earth that reflects the wholeness, perfection, and completion of heaven. This is a lifelong work for all of us. If you can see earthly treasures as a reflection of heavenly treasure, then you can bring a little heaven to your corner of the world.

Money is energy. A powerful symbol, it is a tool that can help you focus your consciousness, grow in understanding, and deal with the motivations of your inner heart. If you say you believe in a generous God, but are stingy or greedy with your material wealth, then you are acting out of disbelief, allowing fear to rule instead of love. If you give too much or inappropriately, you are also acting out of a belief that God or others must be bribed and that poverty is more spiritual than prosperity.

A true spirituality of money is based on the law of giving and receiving. As energy, money must keep moving, and the ability to both give and receive must stay in balance. Giving and receiving allow the flow of energy to move freely. When you allow fear to block the movement of money energy, then you prevent God from being your provider.

Manifesting abundance and creating a healthier relationship with money is not just about the money itself, it's an attitude toward life. As you work to nurture the essentials of the heart in your financial life, you'll discover that it spreads to your entire life experience.

The Golden Rule says: Do unto others as you would have done unto you. The Leaden Rule says: Do unto others before they do unto you. It is built on scarcity, fear, and rivalry, an outer-directed focus that measures self-worth by what you have in comparison to others. The Golden Rule is built on sharing, service, and love. It's an inner-directed way of being that is based on generosity and kindness, creating a mentality of abundance.

You are either declaring abundance or scarcity in your thoughts, choices, and actions. You choose, you decide. When you hold onto what you currently have too tightly, you are putting your faith in that as your supply. When you release money and resources, then you demonstrate your trust in God as your supply. Abundance comes from within, not without. It flows from the attitude of your heart. An attitude of abundance will eventually create an outer manifestation of abundance, no matter what outer circumstances seem to be.

Watch out! Be on your guard against all kinds of greed;
a man's life does not consist in the abundance of his possessions.

—LUKE 12:5 (NIV)

There is less in this than meets the eye.

—TALLULAH BANKHEAD

If I had known what it would be like to have it all,
I might have been willing to settle for less.

—LILY TOMLIN

When you come right down to it,
the secret of having it all is loving it all.

—DR. JOYCE BROTHERS

The health of the apple tells the health of the tree.
You must begin with your own life-giving lives.
It's who you are, not what you say and do, that counts.
Your true being brims over into true words and deeds.

—LUKE 6:44-45 (THE MESSAGE)

Take an attitude check to see if you're following the Golden Rule or living the Leaden Rule. You'll see that a prosperous attitude balances between the extremes. Start by asking yourself these questions:

1. Do I always expect something for nothing?

Or do I give too much, too soon?

No matter where you go, be willing to pay your way. To want something for nothing violates the law of giving and receiving. Give money, energy, time, attention, gratitude. Be conscious of the gifts others bring. At the same time, don't overgive. If you are always giving more than your fair share, if you find yourself playing the martyr and expecting that your giving will "buy" what you want from others, then balance more toward receiving. Try to create a two-way flow between equals instead of an unbalanced contract between superior and inferior.

There is nothing wrong with people possessing riches.
The wrong comes when riches possess people.

—BILLY GRAHAM

2. Am I a bargain hunter?

Or do I overspend and go into debt?

Cheap things bring cheap returns. Underselling, undercutting, bankruptcy, dishonesty, deception, and cheating are all a form of stealing, creating a lower vibration of scarcity instead of a higher vibration of abundance. Help others make a fair profit. Give generously, spend wisely. An occasional bargain can be like a gift, but if you are consistently seeking bargains, then you are in the mindset of wanting something for nothing. In that mindset you know the cost of everything, but the worth of nothing. Debting and overspending are the flip side of being cheap. Balanced generosity is a key to creating an atmosphere of abundance.

If you want to feel rich,
just count all the things you have that money can't buy.

—ANONYMOUS

3. Do I begrudge spending money? Do I hate to pay my bills?

Do I charge too much? Do I cheat others? Am I greedy?

God loves a cheerful giver. Release your money cheerfully, knowing that the law of giving and receiving will replace it and more. Tightening the purse strings can be like closing a faucet. When you pinch the flow, you limit the supply. These attitudes are like the Dead Sea and the Sea of Galilee. The Dead Sea has streams flowing into it but there is no outlet, so it is a salty waste with little life. The Sea of Galilee has fresh water flowing in and out, and it is full of fish and life. Following the law of giving and receiving turns your life into a Sea of Galilee, rich with abundant life.

We should give as we would receive, cheerfully, quickly, and without hesitation;
for there is no grace in a benefit that sticks to the fingers.

—SENECA

4. Do I cling to the past: people, places, things, situations, and belief systems?

Do I focus too much on the future, throwing the baby out with the bath water?

The point of power is in the present. If you are unwilling to let go of the past and refuse to make room for the new, you impoverish yourself. Yet it is also important to value the past and draw wisdom from it. Don't waste energy blaming the past or living for the future. The real question is not "how did I get here?" but "what can I do in this moment to create the life I desire in the future?"

My philosophy is that not only are you responsible for your life,
but doing the best at this moment puts you in the best place for the next moment.

—OPRAH WINFREY

The mind is like a parachute. It works best when it is open.

—ANONYMOUS

5. Do I constantly create chaos and drama?

Do I withdraw, withhold, and keep a cool distance?

There are many ways to avoid intimacy and our own creativity and fulfillment. In *The Artist's Way*, Julia Cameron counsels artists in creative recovery to "Keep the drama on the stage." Isn't it amazing how much drama we can create to avoid the very things we desire the most? Debt, toxic religious agendas, pleasing people, withdrawing from others, detouring in work and in relationships, settling for less than the best—these are just a few of the ways we create drama. The drama can be in the fireworks started by a charismatic crazymaker, but there are also subtle versions of the same thing, even in seemingly serene lives.

If you find yourself continually involved in complex situations in which you have a starring role (and everyone else functions as a bit player), you may be too attached to your own personal drama and judgments. If you find yourself creating the same situation over and over—same script, different players—you may be unconsciously trying to control life or others. A too detached coolness is another way to deal with self-judgment, playing it safe by keeping to yourself and never taking any risks.

If you are caught up in judgment of yourself or others, you may find yourself playing the martyr or telling yourself that you are unique in your suffering.

Phrases like these will keep surfacing over and over: "Everyone always uses me." "Everyone always abandons me." "I can never have/do/be enough." "If only they would . . ."

Remember that we are all unique, yet we are also all the same. Our suffering is both personal and universal. Our gifts are both unique and an expression of the whole. Holding life with an open hand creates space for abundance to grow, while trying to control or manipulate life closes down on the energy of prosperity and well-being. Dramatic fireworks and icy withholding are both attempts to control and manipulate life and other people.

In the end, all the drama and chaos, all the chilly distances, are only excuses to avoid your own potential. Sometimes you can be more afraid of your own greatness than you are of failure and frustration. To move into success and prosperity requires a new story and a new way of defining who you are. It takes courage to let go of old patterns of drama and crazymaking, to write a new script for your life. But once you are aware of the mental games you play, you can also see that you have a choice, and you can create a more benign and loving script that creates a life you enjoy living.

Angels can fly because they take themselves so lightly.

—G. K. CHESTERTON

No one is asking you to leap.
That's just drama, and, for the purpose of creative recovery,
drama belongs on the page or on the canvas or in the clay or in the acting class
or in the act of creativity, however small.

—JULIA CAMERON

What happens when we live God's way? He brings gifts into our lives,
much the same way that fruit appears in an orchard—
things like affection for others, exuberance about life, serenity.
We develop a willingness to stick with things,
a sense of compassion in the heart,
and a conviction that a basic holiness permeates things and people.
We find ourselves involved in loyal commitments.

—GALATIANS 5:22 (THE MESSAGE)

No trumpets sound when the important decisions of our lives are made.
Destiny is made known silently.

—AGNES DE MILLE

Spiritual energy brings compassion in the real world.
With compassion, we see benevolently our own human condition
and the condition of our fellow beings.
We drop prejudice. We withhold judgement.

—CHRISTINA BALDWIN

Once you get rid of the idea that you must please other people before
you please yourself, and you begin to follow your own instincts—
only then can you be successful.
You become more satisfied, and when you are,
other people tend to be satisfied by what you do.

—RAQUEL WELCH

The love of our neighbor in all its fullness simply means being able to say to him,
"What are you going through?"

—SIMONE WEIL

True kindness presupposes the faculty of imagining as one's own the suffering and joys of others.

—ANDRÉ GIDE

Don't hit back; discover beauty in everyone.
If you've got it in you, get along with everybody.

—ROMANS 12:17-18 (THE MESSAGE)

6. Do I make my investments in scarcity? Or do I invest in prosperity?

Look for ways to invest in good things that create abundance and joy for others. Do not invest in that which brings misery and suffering. If you buy a stock because you think it will do well because others are afraid or losing, then it is an investment in scarcity. If you invest in a company that does good and creates a better world, then you are investing in abundance.

Invest your energy as well as your money. Spend your time, treasure, and talents for the things that help create a more abundant and prosperous world.

When you give, see that you give that which multiplies in giving.

—RAYMOND LULL

If you give money, spend yourself with it.

—HENRY DAVID THOREAU

7. What do I trust as my supply? What I see? Or what I cannot see?

Look to the Creator, not the creature as your supply. When you trust in others or in your current circumstances, you limit God's options. You are believing only what you see. But when you open your options by trusting in God as your source, you'll soon see what you dare to believe. Visible resources are limited, but the invisible resources of the Universe are unlimited.

Quantum physics says that there is manifestation: the particle that is the building block of the visible world. And then there is potentiality: the wave that is the invisible—unlimited and containing all that could possibly be. Though the planets and stars and earth seem so vast, compared to the possibilities within the Source that holds all things together, manifestation is only a tiny fraction of that potential.

So it is with your life. What you can see is only a small fraction of the potential you contain. Instead of assuming that God is limited by your understanding, allow your understanding to be expanded by the infinite wisdom of the Creator who designed an elegant Universe that delivers what we desire in surprising and delightful ways.

Some things have to be believed to be seen.

—RALPH HODGSON

Faith is to believe what we do not see;
the reward of this faith is to see what we believe.

—SAINT AUGUSTINE

No eye has seen,
no ear has heard,
no mind has conceived
what God has prepared
for those who love him.

—I CORINTHIANS 2:9 (NIV)

All I have seen teaches me to trust the Creator
for all I have not seen.

—RALPH WALDO EMERSON

8. Do I choose to believe in an abundant universe of love?

Will I choose to invest my life and my resources in a spirit of love?

Life is always a choice between fear and love. When you choose to act out of a loving trust in an abundant universe, you create greater abundance for all. It is your choice. You can contribute to the economy of love and abundance, or put your trust in fear and scarcity. Each choice you make helps to create and perpetuate your experience. It may seem like a leap of faith to invest in love, but the rewards are incalculable.

I firmly believe that if you follow a path that interests you,
not to the exclusion of love, sensitivity, and cooperation with others,
but with the strength of conviction that you can move others by your own efforts,
and do not make success or failure the criteria by which you live,
the chances are you'll be a person worthy of your own respect.

—NEIL SIMON

TAMING THE MONEY DRAGON

Perhaps all the dragons of our lives are princesses
who are only waiting to see us once beautiful and brave.

—RAINER MARIA RILKE

Money problems can be like fire-breathing dragons, demanding that you sacrifice a virgin (like a new idea, a dream, a possibility) to keep the money monster in the dark cave happy. All your worst fears are hiding there in the unexplored darkness. But the day must finally come when you play the part of Saint George and face the dragon. And perhaps, when you bring that fire-breathing dragon to light, he may only be a child's dream, like Puff the Magic Dragon. In the light of day, you may discover that the dragon in the cave is the not merely a source of pain and fear, but a source of great power—if you're willing to acknowledge the shadow so it can be integrated into a life of wholeness.

My mother has a saying. When she faces down a fear, she'll tell me, "I slayed a dragon today." Becoming conscious in the area of money may mean facing a few dragons. But it is all a part of the hero's journey.

I attended an Edwene Gaines workshop on abundance and prosperity. She's a pistol. And an inspiration. I want to be as bold and brave and wonderful when I'm sixty-five. She's rappelled, done hang gliding, and taken trips to Peru and Ecuador to study with shamans, as well as leading fire walking ceremonies at her retreat center. She says that once a year she chooses to do something she's afraid of (like jumping off two-story buildings into the arms of strangers) to make herself face her fears and move beyond them.

Looking at her you'd think she was just another Southern lady who cooks for church suppers. But she's one of the most colorful people you could ever hope to meet. And she definitely pulls no punches. She says that it is entirely possible to change your patterns of lack and fear and scarcity. She suggests that being in debt and living in scarcity are often a socially acceptable way of punishing ourselves. We don't believe we deserve good things, so we make sure we don't get them. Edwene (and many other teachers and mystics) say that such punishing views are a reflection of our self-hatred and a refusal to receive the love and acceptance that God wishes to shower on us.

Ask yourself: Am I punishing myself unconsciously? Do I say I believe in a God of abundance but live like I believe in a God of judgment and scarcity? Am I willing to believe better things of God and myself—and to prepare myself to receive? Along with emphasizing tithing to that which spiritually nurtures and feeds you, Edwene also talks about forgiveness and gratitude. And believing in miracles.

Reading books and doing it on your own may only take you so far. All the money books recommend having a financial advisor, so consider taking a class on money or going to a financial counselor if you are struggling with debt or wondering how to spend your money wisely. If you've been unconscious in your money habits, it may feel horrible to know that someone's going to see how bad it is, but there's also a feeling of relief. Like going to the doctor to get a diagnosis of the pain you've been denying for so long, going to a financial counselor or consultant will help you create a healthier relationship with money and prosperity.

Oy. This can be an area of great resistance. It all sounds so easy and sensible, but to actually do all these things can make you want to go back to sleep, like a little child. Wake up and deal with money issues? Ick. But of course, that too is part of the pattern. How do you avoid the issue? By going back to sleep. How do you solve the problem? By choosing to wake up and deal with it.

Face it instead of denying, stuffing, or fighting it. Even if you don't like what you're looking at, you have to know exactly where you stand. If you want to move out of dangerous territory, you need to know where you are on the map so you can find your way into safer territory.

If you're tired of living a financial life of quiet desperation, take one small step to make a positive change. I have listed resources and books to help you in the back of this book. They can help start you on the path to financial fitness so you can create a life of integrity and elegant simplicity.

Simplicity is . . . being able to take care of
my financial obligations with ease.

The Inexhaustible Resource of Spirit is equal to every demand.
There is no reality in lack.
Abundance is here and now manifest.

—CHARLES FILLMORE

The heart is like a garden. It can grow compassion or fear; resentment or love.
What seeds will you plant there?

—BUDDHA

Fear is worse than the ordeal itself.

—YIDDISH PROVERB

Why is everyone hungry for more?
"More, more," they say. "More, more."
I have God's more-than-enough.

—PSALM 4:6 (THE MESSAGE)

LIVING FOR THE LOVE OF IT: CREATING ENERGY

Without energy life is merely a latent possibility.
The world belongs to the energetic.

—RALPH WALDO EMERSON

Positive attitudes give you more energy. Have you ever felt drained after being around someone who was negative and complaining? Have you ever drained your own energy by imagining worst case scenarios or whining about the things you can't change? On the other hand, have you ever lost track of time doing something you loved to do, and found you weren't tired even after hours of labor? You can generate more of the energy you need to create a life you enjoy by choosing to do things you love and dwelling on the positive. Choose to live life for the love of it and you'll love your life.

Simple small choices can make a big difference in your energy level. From adjusting your attitude to taking care of your body, here are some suggestions for cultivating more energy in your life.

- ❖ In the morning, set your intention to make every day a good day. Affirm that you are connected with a Higher Power and that you are going to draw on that Source of energy for the entire day. Attitudes of faith and optimism can increase your energy levels, while imagined scenarios of doom and gloom will drag you down. When a day seems overwhelming, take it one moment at a time. During a hectic time, say to yourself "I have enough for this minute. I am enough here and now." Practice being in the moment, and allow each moment to carry you through. Affirmations for your day can include: "I have abundant energy and vitality." "Today is a good day and I'm thankful to be alive." "I have everything I need and more." "I love every moment of my life." "I am divinely led throughout every moment of my day."

❖ Breathe deeply, allowing the breath to move you. Donna Farhi, author of *The Breathing Book*, tells us that the breath is like a tide, moving in and out. She says, "If the movement of the breath is restricted or distorted in some way, all other patterns of our movement and consciousness will be restricted or distorted." Do you often find yourself breathing quick and shallow breaths? This kind of breathing stems from and creates tension. Relax your body and calm your nerves by taking deep breaths that reach down deep into the belly.

Breathing deeply allows not only oxygen into our bodies, but also movement. To take a deep breath, then exhale fully with a gentle sigh, helps the body to relax, which will then lead the mind into a more flexible and open state. When we hold our breath, we restrict movement, which becomes a way to control life and resist change. We are in effect saying that we do not want to be moved. "Breathing freely is a courageous act," comments Donna Farhi. "What we discover is that our desire for stasis, our clinging to the life we know, and our bending of every situation to the security of our mental constructs are the very things that destroy our creativity and ability to live freely." Take a deep breath and draw in the energy and renewal you need. Exhale, and release that which no longer serves you. In her jewel of a book on inner and outer beauty, *Lit from Within*, author Victoria Moran reminds us to "walk proudly, breathe fully, and remember who you are."

- Eat a good breakfast. Yes, it's the kind of old-fashioned advice you got from your mom. And it's still good advice. A healthy breakfast fuels you for the day and helps you avoid that mid-morning slump.
- Drink plenty of water. Water replenishes and cleanses your system. It's amazing how a simple glass of water can clear your thinking, balance your appetite, and give you refreshing energy.
- Take regular stress breaks during the day. Dr. Bob Arnot recommends that you hydrate, walk, and/or deep breathe during these time-outs.

Ten-to-fifteen-minute breaks every hour and a half to two hours can keep you alert and energetic throughout a busy work day.

- Spend time in silence and solitude. A morning meditation, a short walk at lunch time, a rendezvous with a hot bath in the evening, writing in your journal before bedtime—any of these can be a time out from the stresses of daily life.
- Make time for fun, especially with friends. If you've been taking life too seriously, you're probably feeling worn around the edges, maybe even edgy. Taking time for play brings you back to center and keeps you balanced in our workaholic society. There's nothing like a good laugh with friends to give you a better perspective on life. Do something you truly love—it will bring you energizing joy.

One filled with joy preaches without preaching.

—MOTHER TERESA

If the sight of the blue skies fills you with joy,
if a blade of grass springing up in the fields has power to move you,
if the simple things of nature have a message that you understand,
rejoice, for your soul is alive.

—ELEANORA DUSE

Simple pleasures that make life worth living:

. . . a friend who invites you to share a walk

. . . mashed potatoes and gravy

. . . grits and gravy (for those born and raised in the South)

. . . heart to heart sharing

. . . whole wheat bread, organic butter, and orange blossom honey

. . . a thoughtful gesture

. . . a single star in a twilight sky

. . . little girls in ruffled dresses

. . . big girls in lace dresses

. . . wilderness preserved

. . . a community gathering

. . . good work to do

. . . lavender essential oil: the Swiss army knife of aromatherapy

. . . a happy soul in a healthy body

. . . a rose garden

. . . birds singing in the branches above

. . . one season giving way to the next

. . . the human heart lifted in prayer and praise

. . . the sound of one instrument exquisitely played

. . . sun warming the skin

. . . the arrow of desire meeting the bull's eye of love

. . . a dog licking your hand

. . . soup simmering on the stove

. . . shade on a hot sunny afternoon

. . . a church potluck

. . . strong arms lifting a heavy burden

. . . gentle hands soothing a frightened child

. . . planting spring bulbs

. . . barns and cows and green fields

. . . picking wild blackberries for a pie

. . . simple honesty and personal accountability

. . . arranging flowers in a vase

. . . a soft dish towel

. . . an artist painting a picture

. . . just "being" with someone you love

Create in Me a Clean Heart

The only way to loose the ties that bind us is by finding freedom from within—
freedom not from circumstances,
but from our conditioned thoughts and emotions.

—PIR VILAYET INAYAT KHAN

BECOMING FULLY PRESENT: CULTIVATING SERENITY

We are fragmented when we wander from our own center.
When our attention is merely reacting to outer events,
or when it is being dominated by something,
it loses contact with its own source.

—KABIR EDMUND HELMINSKI

When the hurricane situations of life buffet us, the storm surges of emotion threaten to overwhelm, and the debris of our fragmented lives swirl around us, it is essential to connect with a deeper, stronger force that is not overwhelmed by the chaos and change of outer events. Coming to the center of ourselves through prayer, meditation, movement, silence, song, dance, and attention to spiritual disciplines can anchor us to a Greater Source. As we learn to cultivate serenity with our attention and intention, we discover there is something within us that has never been cut off from God, and that there is a silent observer who stands above the storms of life. This observer is always within us, always cradling us in a greater reality beyond our human experience on this earth. It is within us, but also felt around us.

The true core of inner simplicity is not the disciplines that bring our attention back to our center, but our connection with the center Itself. Every mystical tradition has its own name for this focused center: Buddha nature, Christ consciousness, presence, awareness, enlightenment, unity, higher self, translucence. It doesn't matter what name you give this experience of wholeness and serene inner connection. You know what it is when you experience it, and you know what it feels like even if you don't have words large enough to define it.

You already know this center. You have experienced it again and again. You may not have understood that it could be cultivated and expanded, or how important it is to creating the life your heart desires to live. You knew this pure clarity as a child, in those times when the world was right and everything seemed to be full of wonder and light. You glimpse this in the transcendent experiences of adulthood as well: a pearly dawn after a night of storms, looking deeply into a lover's eyes, hearing the first cry of a newborn child, and the unmediated innocence of an animal's affection. It is like a sigh of relief as you come in from the cold, shedding wet winter clothes and entering a warm firelit room where love is waiting to embrace you. These small momentary connections with the eternal are available to you all the time, but most of the time you may be too distracted to pay attention.

Yet it is in paying attention, focusing your awareness, and cultivating the sense of connection that these experiences hint at that will develop your capacity for greater and more sustained experiences of centeredness and inner serenity. The more you can quiet the monkey-mind chatter and set ego agendas aside, the more you are able to experience the spiritual depths and inner power that bring focus and creative energy to your outer life.

So choosing simplicity becomes more than merely rearranging your outer life into a more tidy package. Simplicity becomes the very nature and essence of your being, moving with an irresistible force from the inner life to the outer life. You are splitting the atom of your own existence and releasing the quantum energies of the Life Force you have always been connected to.

You discover as you do this that it feels like waking up. Instead of a kaleidoscope of conflicting impressions and out-of-control life events, you begin to discern an order within the chaos. You experience a quickened ability to focus your awareness, set your intention, and allow the power that flows from those choices to bring your outer existence into order and clarity.

Instead of merely rearranging the same pieces of your life into some sort of order, you create whole new options and opportunities to express your deeper nature and generate an entirely different and more beautiful quality of life than you ever dreamed possible. When you learn to calm the storm within, you may discover that you have also learned how to walk on water.

Simplicity is . . . contemplating the eternal in the earthly.

You must learn to be still in the midst of
activity and to be vibrantly alive in repose.

—INDIRA GANDHI

Stay in the center of the circle and
let all things take their course.

—LAO TZU

I thank God for my handicaps, for through them
I have found myself, my work, and my God.

—HELEN KELLER

Spiritual practice is about transformation, but it's also,
and more importantly, about working with what is.

—ANGEL KYODO WILLIAMS

Liberty, when it begins to take root,
is a plant of rapid growth.

—GEORGE WASHINGTON

There is a part of every living thing that wants to become itself.
The tadpole into the frog, the chrysalis into the butterfly,
a damaged human being into a whole one.
That is spirituality.

—ELLEN BASS

Everything in life is pointing us
back to our true nature.

—STEPHEN COPE

There is a secret one inside us;
the planets like galaxies pass through his hands like beads.

—KABIR

We feel and know that we are eternal.

—EDMUND SPENCER

True contentment is a real, even an active virtue—
not only affirmative but creative.
It is the power of getting out of any situation all there is in it.

—G. K. CHESTERTON

We look backward too much and we look forward too much;
thus we miss the only eternity of which we can be absolutely sure—
the eternal present, for it is always now.

—WILLIAM PHELPS

I was sitting, wondering what I should do,
when I received this revelation;
Open your heart.
Feel the closeness with God.
Look inside yourself.
Tend the awareness there.

—BAHAUDDIN

Between stimulus and response,
there is a space.
In that space lies our freedom
and our power to choose our response.
In our response lies our growth
and our happiness.

—AUTHOR UNKNOWN

When you live completely today there is a
great intensity in it and in its beauty.

—KRISHNA

It is very important, especially while you are young, to love something with your whole being—a tree, an animal, your teacher, your parent—for then you will find out for yourself what it is to love without conflict, without fear.

—J. KRISHNAMURTI

There is no place where the Presence of God is not,
only people who are not fully present in the places where they are.
You have only to be present to know all you need to know.

—KEN CAREY

ENTERING THE PEACEABLE KINGDOM: MOVING BEYOND ANGER

We are what we practice.
If we become angry a lot, then essentially we are practicing anger.
And we become quite good at it.
Conversely, if we practice being joyful, then a joyful person is what we become.

—AURAM DAVIS

Anger is energy, and most of the time we misdirect our energy. If you spend your energy complaining, pointing the finger of blame, and concentrating on who's "right" and what's "wrong" instead of working to heal the situation, you're draining away the creative energy it takes to solve the problem. Instead of being a catalyst for change, anger becomes an excuse for staying stuck.

Letting go of anger, self-pity, and self-righteousness can be a powerful decision. It runs counter to our society's emphasis on who's "right" and who's "wrong." For example, the so-called "culture wars" usually seem to be about establishing one point of view as superior, rather than being open to new ideas and alternative insights. A lot of anger is generated and energy is wasted in such either/or thinking. Pundits and talking heads on TV add to the problem, offering sound-bite arguments pro or con, but never really taking time to communicate, examine things in-depth, or listen with real empathy. Our political situation feeds the either/or, win/lose mentality as well, creating power structures that cater to those who use adversarial approaches to dealing the issues of the day. Anger becomes essential to maintaining power, and an angry response to the injustices that inevitably follow the amassing of power is assured.

This dynamic is reflected in the microcosm of personal relationships as well as the macrocosm of societal ills. How often does personal anger emerge from an imbalance of power, with one person being the "oppressor" whose might makes right and the other person playing the role of the "victim" who feels powerless and stifled? Such either/or thinking and role playing is also a dead end.

True power is not found in the dance of betrayer and betrayed. Pinning blame or saying "If only he would change . . ." or "When they realize how wrong they are . . ." or "I'll show them . . ." wastes precious creative energy. Even depression can be a form of anger, turning anger inward, crushing the spirit under the weight of disappointment and learned helplessness. We have the power to unlearn our angry ways and exchange our victim stories for empowering visions of who we are and what we can become.

My journey out of anger began with recognizing that I had a pattern of anger. I realized that under my exterior persona of sweetness and light an angry woman was constantly counting wrongs committed—or at the very least things that I didn't agree with. I might smile and say some soothing platitude, but there was a constant stream of criticism, anger, and judgment going on beneath the light-filled surface. I might try to deny the shadows of anger, but that only made them stronger and darker. I created a core story that either cast me in the role of victim or in the role of potential savior. Either "they" were oppressing me or I had to "fix" the problem. I would tell myself the same story over and over, rehearsing rights and wrongs in my mind. While it might have been true that others did indeed do wrong and hurtful things, my continual focus on their wrongdoing gave me permission to avoid my own responsibility in the situation. My anger and blame only contributed to the cycle of wrong, generating more bad energy and no real solutions.

It was when I decided to make a few simple changes that I began to come to terms with my pattern of anger and learned to move beyond it. I discovered a quiet, childlike spirit as I cleared anger from my life, a silent non-judging presence that offered a quiet refuge from the storms of anger and frustrated expectations. I saw many of the frustrations and failures of my life dissipate, even if they didn't seem directly related to my anger. I had more energy to give to creative projects, was able to think more clearly, and enjoy more loving interaction with others. I didn't realize how much energy had been wasted on maintaining my anger until I stopped feeding it.

Here are a few of the insights I gained as I came to terms with my pattern of anger:

- I recognized that no matter how I got into a situation, what mattered most was not assigning blame but deciding that I could take responsibility for my own thoughts and actions, no matter what part I played in the situation. I couldn't control what the other person said or did, but I could choose my response, decide to have a different reaction, and make better choices.
- I also understood that even the smallest choice could either enhance or take away my personal power. Whatever the wrong, I could choose a negative reaction that would chain me to the problem as it existed, or I could choose a positive response that opened the door to new options.
- I had to let go of my story of who was right, who was wrong. Instead of playing the same scenarios over and over in my mind, I let go of my limited view of the situation and opened my heart to create a quiet space

so that something new could emerge from the chaos of my angry feelings. Suspending judgment and letting go of the old story was such a relief. I discovered that my energies could be better used to create a new story instead of wasted defending the old story.

- Consciously choosing to replace negative angry thoughts with positive thoughts and affirmations took discipline, but also helped me to direct my energies into more constructive channels.
- Acknowledging that I didn't really have all the answers left space for God to bring new insights and options into the situation. Affirmative prayers, positive attitudes, and taking things moment by moment opened a space for God to walk into the room and grace to work in unexpected and miraculous ways. I often found that the frustrating situation resolved itself or that it really wasn't as important as it had seemed when I was so consumed with my own anger.
- I began to focus on what I wanted instead of what I didn't want. Instead of going over old stories and disappointments, I began to imagine what life could be like if all things were working together for the highest good. I challenged myself to explore other options and feed my soul with life-affirming activities and ideas. I put my energy into creating good and saw the good multiply and the bad diminish.

- I was willing to forgive others—and myself. I acknowledged that we were all doing the best we knew how to do with what we had to work with at the time. I acknowledged that I had the power to make better choices now, and that taking the high road was the best choice I could make in each moment.
- Finally, I learned to release my expectations to God, choosing forgiveness and trusting that there was a greater power that could transform and heal in ways my ego-based planning could never anticipate. I looked to God to be my source of good, not other people. I chose to trust that God could bring good out of the most unpromising situation. I exchanged my limited view for God's unlimited grace and mercy and love.

I'm no angel. I still get angry, especially when I read headlines or experience something that is unfair or unkind. There are always good reasons to get angry, still injustices to be made right and battles to fight. But now I choose my battles consciously, acknowledging anger as a servant who warns me of trouble, but not allowing anger to master me. I know that inner peace and stillness are much more powerful than the red raging bull of anger.

I choose to focus on creating what I desire instead of criticizing what I don't like. I have the power to choose my response. I only give them power over me when I do not maintain power over myself. Anger only rules in my heart when I choose to practice anger instead of practicing peace.

I have let go of having to be a victim or a savior. I do not need to be rescued and I do not need to rescue others. God is my source of good, and God can bring my good to me in many ways, as long as I am willing to receive it. God can bring good to others, if they choose to allow their good to come to them. God is greater than circumstances may indicate, and so I can trust that even a frustrating, negative situation holds the seed of triumph, even if I do not yet see its fruit. I choose to make myself available to the creative energies within, releasing my anger and making space for something new to emerge. I have found that something new always does arrive in Divine timing, like the still small voice of God that whispers after the storm has passed by.

Simplicity is . . . a peaceful heart and quiet spirit.

And behold, the Lord passed by, and a great and strong wind rent the mountains,
and broke in pieces the rocks before the Lord, but the Lord was not in the wind;
and after the wind was an earthquake, but the Lord was not in the earthquake;
and after the earthquake a fire, but the Lord was not in the fire;
and after the fire a still small voice.

—I KINGS 19:11-12 (RSV)

An angry person is full of poison.

—CONFUCIUS

Anger and intolerance are the twin enemies of correct understanding.

—MAHATMA GANDHI

He who angers you, conquers you.

—PROVERB

If you are patient in one moment of anger,
you will avoid a hundred days of sorrow.

—CHINESE PROVERB

Slowness to anger makes for deep understanding;
a quick-tempered person stockpiles stupidity.

—PROVERBS 14:29 (THE MESSAGE)

You cannot acquire the gift of peace if by your anger
you destroy the peace of the Lord.

—GREGORY THE GREAT

Everyone should be quick to listen, slow to speak, and slow to become angry,
for man's anger does not bring about the righteous life God desires.

—JAMES 1:19-20 (NIV)

Life appears to me too short to be spent in
nursing animosity or registering wrong.

—CHARLOTTE BRONTË

Holding onto anger is like grasping a hot coal with the intent of throwing it at someone else; you are the one who gets burned.

—BUDDHA

I never have any difficulty believing in miracles, since I experienced the miracle of a change in my own heart.

—SAINT AUGUSTINE

Our work is to cross a threshold into emptiness and stillness. It is like entering an empty room that proves to hold a great presence. The apparent emptiness of simple presence is richer than the crowded experience of ordinary personality. We can either be empty with Spirit or full of ourselves.

—KABIR EDMUND HELMINSKI

The significant problems in life cannot be solved at the same level of thinking which created them.

—ALBERT EINSTEIN

Should I encounter chaos, conflict, or confusion,
I go within and find the clarity to see any situation exactly as it is.
I see the good and the love in all concerned.
I find the wisdom to resolve any issues and the willingness
to release all I cannot remedy.
I know I can live in the appearance of chaos without letting it live in me,
and I move through any conflict without letting it move into me.
I choose to live a life of peace and harmony.

—BILL THOMPSON

FORGIVING OURSELVES AND OTHERS: OBSERVING OUR JUDGEMENTS

Explore the possibilities of forgiveness and surrender. Notice that it is not the unforgiven person who suffers but the unforgiving one. Notice also that surrender liberates you from trying to change what cannot be changed.

—ROGER JAHNKE

Forgiveness is letting go. Just as you chose to get rid of old things and ideas that were cluttering your life, so you can choose to release the resentments and judgments that still bind you to old ways of being.

Forgiveness is not forgetting, nor is it denying what happened or your feelings about it. Neither does forgiveness excuse another person for his or her actions. Forgiveness is a conscious choice to release the past and trust that God has better ways to make things right. Even if the other party does not express regret or acknowledge the wrong, you need to forgive. Give it as an unconditional gift. Forgiveness is about you, not about them. It is none of your business what they do with it. Though you may experience a reconciliation, the choice to forgive is something you do for yourself. Forgiveness is good for you. Holding onto resentment and unforgivingness is like drinking poison and expecting it to kill the other person. Choosing to forgive is part of a sustained commitment to yourself. It is a choice to live a life free of unwanted emotional baggage.

As you review what happened and the emotional pain it caused you, forgiveness begins with the decision to heal and let go of the past. Then you must choose to change your own mind. That means changing how you think about what happened and seeing it from a higher perspective. *A Course in Miracles* says that forgiveness is realizing that what you thought happened really didn't happen. The choice to forgive opens the way to see into the heart of what was happening, something you could not understand when you were in the midst of the painful event. When you see the spiritual truth hidden in the material reality, you can begin to find personal meaning and unexpected wisdom that grew out of the situation that caused you so much pain. It is your choice to release the past that makes room for good to come out of a bad situation. With this awareness, you can begin to move on.

I have found this to be true in my own life. When I made a conscious choice to take the high road by honoring myself and refusing to hold resentment,

I realized that the person or situation that had been so hurtful offered me an opportunity to make another choice and take another path of personal evolution. We teach each other lessons we don't want to learn. When I remained obstinate in my unforgivingness, I stayed stuck in the same mind-set that created the difficulty in the first place. I could choose instead to see the person who hurt me as a healing angel offering the opportunity to change an old pattern. Time did prove that forgiving was the most healing and empowering thing I could do. I grew because of those decisions to take the high road. By honoring myself and by choosing forgiveness, I was freed of the past and of the necessity to create similar situations again.

If you keep experiencing the same bad situations over and over, life is offering you another opportunity to make a different choice. If you hear yourself saying "Why does this keep happening to me?" it's time to look at the ways you might have contributed to the problem and perhaps even set yourself up for it. I'm coming to believe that we create these situations on a soul level so that we can grow and evolve. If you keep choosing the old ways of reacting, then you'll keep creating the same old situations, only they'll get more and more difficult each time around. If you decide to make a more conscious and loving choice, honoring yourself and the other person to the best of your ability and understanding, then you will outgrow the need for such situations. As time goes by, you'll also be able to see the dynamics of the situation more clearly, because by taking responsibility for your choices, you'll understand what those choices really meant.

Forgiveness is a process. Some days you'll feel sure that you've released all the old feelings of guilt, anger, and resentment. Other days, something will surface and the wound will feel as fresh and raw as if it were only yesterday that the offense occurred. You must consciously choose to forgive. Ask God to help you do this, and you will receive the help you need. If you are willing to surrender your pain, you will be healed. Your intuition will guide you, and over time you'll learn how to live free of the old resentments and pain, able to give your energy to creating abundance and joy.

Forgiveness is a lifelong habit that must be consciously chosen again and again. As you learn to forgive, you'll come to understand that the person who most needs forgiveness is you. You can't be honest with yourself, or accept both the light and the shadow without forgiving. Understand that everyone, including you, was doing the best they could with what they had to work with at the time. After you've done your work of forgiveness, and if needed, made restitution, you can release the past and go on with your life, a wiser and better person than if you had never gone through that experience. Forgiveness is an essential part of the curriculum in the school of life.

It is said that in a certain tribe in Africa, when a woman becomes pregnant she goes out into the wilderness to pray and listen until she hears the song of the child she bears within. Then she teaches the song to the other members of the tribe, and they sing it when the baby is born and throughout the lifetime of that member of the tribe. They sing the song when the child becomes an adolescent, when the adult is married, and at the time of parting and death. But there is one other time that the tribe sings this song, and this is when one member of the tribe has caused suffering to another member of the tribe. Then they gather in a circle and set him in the center. They sing his song to remind him not of the wrong done, but of his own beauty and potential. When a child loses the way, it is love and not punishment that brings the lost one home.

Simplicity is . . . forgiving and moving on with your life.

Simplicity is . . . singing the true song of the heart.

All nature is alive, awake, and aware with the divine presence,
and everything in life responds to the song of the heart.

—ERNEST HOLMES

When I have forgiven myself and remembered who I am,
I will bless everyone and everything I see.

—A COURSE IN MIRACLES

I like to think the day you were born you were given
the whole world as your birthday present.

—LEO BUSCAGLIA

Surely you desire truth in the inner parts;
you teach me wisdom in the inmost place.

—PSALM 51:6 (NIV)

For our creativity does not consist in being right all the time
but in making of all our experiences, including the apparently
mistaken and imperfect ones, a holy whole.

—MATTHEW FOX

If you want to see the brave, look at those who can forgive.
If you want to see the heroic, look at those who can love in return for hatred.

—BHAGAVAD GITA

The great epochs in our lives are at the points when we gain the courage
to rebaptize our badness as the best in us.

—NIETZSCHE

Experience is not what happens to you;
it is what you do with it that happens to you.

—ALDOUS HUXLEY

There is no past we can bring back by longing for it.
There is only an eternal now that builds and creates out of the past
something new and better.

—GOETHE

Sin is an obstruction in the heart; an inability to feel and comprehend
all that is noble, true, and great, and to take part in the good.

—THE TALMUD

Peace is more important than all justice; and peace was not made for justice, but justice made for the sake of peace.

—MARTIN LUTHER KING, JR

In prayer there is a connection between what God does and what you do. You can't get forgiveness from God, for instance, without also forgiving others. If you refuse to do your part, you cut yourself off from God's part.

—MATTHEW 6:14-15 (THE MESSAGE)

The weak can never forgive. Forgiveness is the attribute of the strong.

—MAHATMA GANDHI

He that cannot forgive others, breaks the bridge over which he himself must pass if he would ever reach heaven; for everyone has need to be forgiven.

—GEORGE HERBERT

Forgiveness is not an occasional act; it is an attitude.

—MARTIN LUTHER KING, JR.

When you forgive, you in no way change the past—
but you sure do change the future.

—BERNARD MELTZER

Without forgiveness, there's no future.

—DESMOND TUTU

The practice of forgiveness is our most important
contribution to the healing of the world.

—MARIANNE WILLIAMSON

FEAR IS THE POISON,
LOVE IS THE ANTIDOTE

Allowing fear to rule your mind will merely make you increasingly fearful,
but keeping control of your mind will keep you unafraid
even when fear boldly approaches you face to face.
A steady mind is the most effective antidote to fear.

—SWAMI KRIPALVANANDA

I know there are many reasons to be afraid in this uncertain world. Old structures are breaking down and we don't yet see what will take their place. We live in a time of upheaval, crisis, and transition.

But I also know this. If we only focus on what's wrong and what's falling apart, it will sap the very energies we need to turn things around. If we spend our energies on criticizing and complaining, we will have no will left to create. If we only judge by the outer appearances, we will not have the wisdom to discern the potential within. The Bible proclaims that love is stronger than death, and this is what I choose to stake my life on.

Human beings made choices and created the world we are now experiencing. We are the ones who are making the choices that will create what will be experienced in the future. Do we want to give up in despair, allowing our fears to overcome our faith? Or are we willing to stake everything on the power of love?

The physicist tells us that we are all connected. If this is true, then if we can raise our consciousness, dare to dream of a better world, and make simple choices each day in love and hope, then we could unleash the potential for quantum change. Anyone who believes in God, prayer, and love can tell you that miracles are possible. I've seen this potential released in my own life, and there are many, many stories of the power of love and prayer and intention that have created hope in the place of hopelessness. Let's make a deliberate choice to focus our energies on better things. We are co-creators with God who can bring about positive change—perhaps more dynamically than we can yet imagine.

In the end, each person must choose. Will you choose fear? Or will you choose love? Fear shrinks back, practices scarcity-thinking, and focuses on the problems of the past, projecting them into the future. Love focuses on the potential for a better future, makes a choice in the here and now believing it will make a positive difference, and knows that God's abundance is ever present for our every need. Every time you choose love, you're making a statement of faith in the creative abilities of the human heart united with a God who can help humanity change the world: one thought, one choice, one action at a time.

Fear is the toxin that paralyzes. Love is the elixir that brings healing and transformation. There are no guarantees that all your dreams will come true, all your problems will be over, or that the world will suddenly become a perfect place. But a cultivated receptivity to love and its expression in this world will create a sacred alchemy that will take you to new levels of consciousness and help you create a better life than could ever be created from a fear-based mentality. I've learned to make choices out of love instead of fear and it has transformed my life. I know it can happen for you, too.

Simplicity is . . . choosing love over fear.

Fear says no. Love says yes.

Fear paralyzes. Love dances in ecstasy.

Fear is based on expectation.
Love is based on intention.

Fear dictates and controls.
Love encourages and improvises.

Fear procrastinates and complains.
Love takes the next step in calm faith.

Fear believes life happens TO you.
Love knows life happens THROUGH you.

Fear believes that what you see is all there is.
Love knows that, with God, all things are possible.

Love is the energizing elixir of the universe,
the cause and effect of all harmonies.

—RUMI

Those who are afraid to make mistakes serve a god of fear.
Their love is incomplete.
Go forth boldly.
Have the courage to live your vision in spite of your fears.

—KEN CAREY

All our failures are ultimately failures in love.

—IRIS MURDOCH

If grass can grow through cement,
love can find you at every time in your life.

—CHER

The future is not waiting for us.
We create it by the power of imagination.

—PIR VILAYAT KHAN

We are all born for love.
It is the principle of existence, and its only end.

—BENJAMIN DISRAELI

Love is letting go of fear.

—GERALD JAMPOLSKY

A loving person lives in a loving world. A hostile person lives in a hostile world.
Everyone you meet is your mirror.

—KEN KEYES JR.

What lies behind us and what lies before us are tiny matters compared to what lies within us.

—RALPH WALDO EMERSON

Transformation *does not mean to fix or make go away whatever trauma and scars you may be carrying from childhood; instead, you slowly develop a new relationship with your difficulty, such that it is no longer a controlling factor in your life.*

—PHILLIP MOFFITT

As Within, So Without

May the outward and inward man be at one.

—SOCRATES

COME AWAY, MY BELOVED: CONNECTING WITH THE ETERNAL

I would like to achieve a state of inner spiritual grace from which I could function and give as I was meant to in the eye of God.

—ANNE MORROW LINDBERGH

In his book *Coaching the Artist Within*, Eric Maisel says that it is essential to find a way to connect to the coach within—that part of you that is wiser and sees your life from a higher perspective. I found a connection to that deeper awareness through journaling. I use Julia Cameron's morning pages format; three pages written longhand first thing in the morning. I have done this since the summer of 1994 when I first started reading her classic, *The Artist's Way*. I had tried to start diaries and journals before, but nothing seemed to stick. But the morning pages took on a life of their own, soon becoming an essential part of my daily routine. I was ready and the inner teacher came.

It took awhile to settle into doing the morning pages on a consistent basis. At first I would write them every other day, or in the evening. But with time, I found that I was settling into a rhythm and the morning pages became an essential start to my day. They set the tone of my morning and helped me focus, allowing me to drain my brain of all the niggling worries and chaotic thoughts that were circling in my mind like crazed crying birds. After awhile, consistent writing seemed to loosen the flow of thoughts and began to bring some sort of order out of chaos. Morning pages became a place to explore new ideas, hash over old arguments, dream about what I desired, denounce what I no longer believed, and generally have an ongoing conversation with myself.

Some days the pages are a whiny collection of complaints, other days brilliant insights flow. Morning pages help me face the things I want to avoid, anchoring me to reality and helping me to stop procrastinating or fantasizing and do something about what needs to be done. They are the place that gives me space to speculate, explore, vent frustrations, acknowledge fears, play with creative ideas, acknowledge my shortcomings, and recognize my strengths. I meet a wiser self in those pages, too. Sometime I access deep wisdom and insight that proves to be wiser than I know at the time of writing. Morning pages are a listening post to hear the whispers of intuition, the guide that uses gut feelings to navigate the shoals of current events. As I work with the morning pages over time, I begin to see patterns and to observe that I might be going over the same old territory in a new situation. I can look back and trace my growth.

I highly recommend doing some sort of morning meditation to begin the day. Whether you journal, read scriptures and pray, do moving meditation like Tai Chi or yoga, walk or run, or write morning pages like I do, creating a regular, ongoing time for quieting your mind can help you connect with a deeper wisdom. I love the morning pages because they leave a trail of thought behind. I write in college-ruled notebooks—not spiralbound because I'm left-handed and my hand rubs against the spiral. I use simple notebooks, usually a five subject style, just so I have more pages to write in before I go to the next notebook. I also create cover collages with pictures and quotes and affirmations that speak to me. I laminate them with self-adhesive lamination paper and clear packing tape. It's fun just to go back to look through the covers. They encourage me still.

If you want to enhance your spiritual and creative growth, I also recommend using the creative tools found in *The Artist's Way* and other books on creativity. Even if you don't consider yourself an official "artist" you are a creative person, and these books can encourage you to live a more creative and satisfying life. For me, morning pages are supplemented by regular walks; at least three times a week at a favorite wild place, more often when time and weather permit. The artist's date, where you take yourself out on a creative junket—visiting a museum, taking in a concert, going to a crafts store, seeing a movie by yourself—is a playful tool that can sometimes be the hardest appointment to keep. I can do work-oriented tasks like journaling, but going out to play ends up low on the priority list. But an artist's play date fills the artist's mind with fresh images and feeds the creative soul. It takes you away from the daily humdrum and reminds you to think out of the box.

I also love to read and I read many spiritual books. I have devotionals to read for the evening before I go to bed. I keep a gratitude journal and fill in five things to be thankful for every evening. Sometimes the page is filled with goodies, other days it's the simple things like bed or birdsong. This is the best journal to go back and read again, for it highlights only the positive things I have experienced. It's wonderful to go back and see that even the most mundane day was rich in God's mercies.

There are many books and resources available to help you find a form of meditation that is meaningful to you. Whether you write in a journal or have a formal prayer time or close your eyes and chant, coming away by yourself to connect within and with God nurtures your soul and becomes a sweet time spent with the Beloved. Art can be spiritual practice, as well as craft, or anything you do with regularity and rhythm. Knitting, gardening, athletics, building, cooking, creating, making—all provide a way to connect with the eternal in the here and now. You can find a piece of heaven on earth when your earthly task allows you to meditate on heavenly things. You will discover an inner spring of living water that will quench your thirst and nourish your soul.

Simplicity is . . . starting the day with meditation.
Simplicity is . . . a prayer in the night.

My memory is in my hands. I can remember things only if I have a pencil and I write with it and I can play with it. I think your hand concentrates for you. I don't know why this should be so.

—DAME REBECCA WEST

Poetry and mysticism both derive from a common source, the ground or depth of the soul, where the Mystery of Being is experienced.

—BEDE GRIFFITHS

What was any art but an effort to make a sheath,
a mold in which to imprison for a moment the shining,
elusive element which is life itself—life hurrying past us and running away,
too strong to stop, too sweet to lose?

—WILLA CATHER

We are shiny, not tarnished; large, not small; beautiful, not damaged—
although we may be ignorant of our grace, power, and dignity.

—JULIA CAMERON

To survive we must begin to know sacredness.
The pace at which most of us live prevents this.

—CHRYSTOS

I am a dancer. I believe that we learn by practice.
Whether it means to learn to dance by practicing dancing
or to learn to live by practicing living, the principles are the same . . .
One becomes in some area an athlete of God.

—MARTHA GRAHAM

Your sacred space is where you can
find yourself again and again.

—JOSEPH CAMPBELL

We receive the light, then we impart it.
Thus we repair the world.

—THE KABBALAH

It is the creative potential itself in human beings
that is the image of God.

—MARY DALY

Artists in each of the arts
seek after and care for nothing but love.

—MARSILIO FICINO

It is in our idleness, in our dreams, that the submerged
truth sometimes comes to the top.

—VIRGINIA WOOLF

To write is to admit.

—KRISTJANA GUNNARS

When the writing starts, listen.

—MARIANNE MOORE

Only one thing is more frightening than speaking your truth.
And that is not speaking.

—NAOMI WOLF

Like an ability or a muscle, hearing your inner wisdom is strengthened by doing it.

—ROBERT GASS

If I have ever made any valuable discoveries, it has been owing more to patient attention, than any other talent.

—ISAAC NEWTON

Painting is just another way of keeping a diary.

—PABLO PICASSO

When Svetaketu, at his father's bidding, had brought a ripe fruit
from the banyan tree, the father said to him,
"Split the fruit in two, dear son."
"Here you are, I have split it in two."
"What do you find there?"
"Innumerable tiny seeds."
"Then take each one of them and split it."
"I have split the seed."
"And what do you find there?"
"Why, nothing, nothing at all."
"Ah, dear son, but this great tree cannot possibly come from nothing. Even if you cannot see with your eyes that subtle something in the seed which produces this mighty form, it is present nonetheless. That is the power, that is the spirit unseen which pervades everywhere and all things. Have faith! This is the spirit which lies at the root of all existence, and that also art thou, O Svetaketu."

—FROM THE *CHANDOGYA UPANISHED*

I believe that God is within me, as the sun is in the color and fragrance of the flower, the Light in my darkness, the Voice in my silence.

—HELEN KELLER

The kingdom of God is within you.

—LUKE 17:21 (NIV)

Prayer is the contemplation of the facts of life from the highest point of view.

—RALPH WALDO EMERSON

Prayer is not an old woman's idle amusement.
Properly understood and applied, it is the most potent instrument of action.

—MAHATMA GANDHI

Prayer is neither black magic nor is it a form of demand note.
Prayer is a relationship. The act of praying is more analogous
to clearing away the underbrush which shuts out a view than it is
to begging on the street. There are many different kinds of prayer.
Yet all prayer has one basic purpose. We pray not to get something,
but to open up a two-way street between us and God,
so that we and others may inwardly become something.

—JOHN HEUSS

May the wisdom of God instruct me,
the eye of God watch over me,
the ear of God hear me,
the word of God give me sweet talk,
the hand of God defend me,
the way of God guide me.

—SAINT PATRICK

To be religious is to give your life so that the world may be
more beautiful, more just, more at peace;
it is to prevent egotistical and self-serving ends from disrupting
this harmony of the whole.

—ARTURO PAOLI

WAKING UP

There is a power in me that knows what to do and how to do it.

—ERNEST HOLMES

One of the most important reasons to practice the art of inner simplicity is to wake up to your own potential for greatness. Every disaster or setback can become a wake-up call. Every choice you make counts. Your imagination is the key that unlocks the yet-to-be created life that is possible for you. Your stillness and serenity create a place for better thoughts to emerge. Your focused intention brings your dreams into manifested reality.

Clearing the clutter of old belief systems and outmoded ways of thinking can produce a whole new sense of freedom and clarity. The inner changes begin to find their reflection in the ordering of the outer life. When you are no longer ruled by fear, anger, or false judgments, you can be open to greater ideas and higher perspectives. You begin to rise above defining yourself by your problems and learn to define yourself by your potential.

As you learn to release that which no longer serves you, you create room for something better to enter. When you understand that you are created for greatness and growth, you begin to realize that you live in a universe of infinite possibilities, and that you are the intersection of time and eternity where those possibilities can become realities. Because you realize you truly do have the choice and the power to change your thoughts, work with instead of against your emotions, and discover creative solutions, you are free to take responsibility for your life in a way you never have before.

You are more capable than you yet realize. There is power in positive thought and co-creative prayer. Your intention and God's providence can create a new pattern of love, joy, and peace in the world, if you are willing to do the inner work. It was one thing to play the victim and to believe yourself powerless. But if indeed you are an intersection of eternity and time, with access to spiritual treasures and potentialities hidden within the human heart, then being a victim or blaming others or giving up is no longer an acceptable option.

No matter how dire circumstances may seem, or how numbing a situation may feel, you have access to infinite resources within. God is with you and has created you for this particular moment in time. You are God's gift to the world, and this is your wake-up call. If you choose to take the high road, you will experience the flow of even greater spiritual resources. But it is your choice. It doesn't matter how you got here. What matters is where you choose to go from here.

You are the gift—your talents are just the channel for that gift to manifest in the world. With a quiet mind and focused intention you can make a tremendous difference in your corner of the world. As you continue to practice inner simplicity you'll be increasingly able to serve. It will be as natural as breathing in and breathing out. You cultivate your potential and in doing so you encourage others to cultivate their own gifts and answer their high calling from God.

The Hopi elders have told us: We are the ones we have been waiting for. The art of simplicity is a small reminder of ways you can begin to clear the clutter of outmoded ways of being and choose to move beyond personal chaos into a fuller unfolding of your God-given potential. The choice is yours. Are you willing to be the light in the world that God created you to be?

Simplicity is . . . creating space for your inner greatness
to unfold and blossom.

Now is the time to know
That all you do is sacred.

—HAFIZ

We will go into the future as a single sacred community,
or we will all perish in the attempt.

—THOMAS BERRY

The higher part of yourself has a "knowing" that you're not alone,
that you go where you're sent, that you'll be guided, that you can surrender,
and that it's going to work out.

—WAYNE DYER

True spirituality is not religion—it is a state of being.

—MARY HESSION

The emotional frontier is truly the next frontier to conquer in ourselves. The opportunity of this time is that we can develop our emotional potential and accelerate rather dramatically into a new state of being.

—DOC CHILDRE AND HOWARD MARTIN

Awake, awake, great ones! the world is burning with misery.
Can you sleep?
Let us call and call till the sleeping gods awake,
till the god within answers the call.
What more is in life? What greater work?

—SWAMI VIVEKANANDA

Awake O Sleeper and rise from the dead . . .

—EPHESIANS 5:14 (AUTHOR'S PARAPHRASE)

There is only one time when it is essential to awaken.

That time is now.

—BUDDHA

Your vision will become clear only when you look into your heart.

Who looks outside, dreams. Who looks inside, awakens.

—CARL JUNG

Spirituality means waking up.
Most people, even though they don't know it, are asleep.
They're born asleep, they live asleep, they marry in their sleep,
they die in their sleep without ever waking up.
They never understand the loveliness and the beauty of
this thing we call human existence.

—ANTHONY DE MELLO

We are not powerless specks of dust drifting around in the wind,
blown by random destiny. We are, each of us, like beautiful snowflakes—
unique, born for a specific reason and purpose.

—ELISABETH KÜBLER-ROSS

Nature never repeats herself
and the possibilities of one human soul will never be found in another.

—ELIZABETH CADY STANTON

There is a vitality, a life-force, a quickening that is translated through you into action, and because there is only one of you in all time, this expression is unique. And if you block it, it will never exist through any other medium and it will be lost—the world will not have it.

—MARTHA GRAHAM

In Hebrew, the words spirituality *and* fragrance *have a shared grammatical origin and are therefore almost identical: the word for "spirit" is* Ruach *and for "scent" is* Reach. *This reflects the ancient belief that sanctity is characterized by divine fragrance.*

—DR. NAOMI PORAN

Everywhere we go, people breathe in the exquisite fragrance.
Because of Christ, we give off a sweet scent rising to God,
which is recognized by those on the way of salvation—
an aroma redolent with life.

—II CORINTHIANS 2:15-16 (THE MESSAGE)

The fragrance of holiness travels even against the wind.

—BUDDHA

I did my best and God did the rest.

—HATTIE MCDANIEL

The purpose of a man's heart are deep waters,
but a man of understanding draws them out.

—PROVERBS 20:5 (NIV)

You can come to understand your purpose in life by slowing down
and feeling your heart's desires.

—MARCIA WEIDER

Every moment comes to you pregnant with divine purpose . . .
Once it leaves your hands and your power to deal with it as you please,
it plunges into eternity, to remain forever what you made it.

—FULTON J. SHEEN

All around us we observe a pregnant creation.
The difficult times of pain throughout the world are simply birth pangs.
But it's not only around us; it's within us.
The Spirit of God is arousing us within.
We're also feeling the birth pangs.
These sterile and barren bodies of ours are yearning for full deliverance.
That is why waiting does not diminish us,
any more than waiting diminishes a pregnant mother.
We are enlarged in the waiting.
We, of course, don't see what is enlarging us.
But the longer we wait, the larger we become,
and the more joyful our expectancy.

—ROMANS 8:22-25 (THE MESSAGE)

When you are inspired by some great purpose,
some extraordinary project,
all your thoughts break their bounds:
your mind transcends limitations,
your consciousness expands in every direction,
and you find yourself in a new, great, and wonderful world.
Dormant forces, faculties, and talents become alive,
and you discover yourself to be a greater person by far
than you ever dreamed yourself to be.

—PATANJALI

As Above, So Below

Thy will be done, thy kingdom come, on earth as it is in heaven.

—FROM THE LORD'S PRAYER, MATTHEW 6:10 (KJV)

SAY YES TO LIFE:
AFFIRMATIVE PRAYER

Just as we plant a seed and walk away from it, nature takes it up,
and the law of its own being evolves it,
so let us believe the same thing about our word—
something takes it up, something evolves it,
and something will make it manifest in our experience.

—ERNEST HOLMES

The first rule of improvisational theater is to say "yes." Answer all questions with a yes. Say yes to everything. Say yes even if it's to something absurd. Say yes and play with it. When you know that your partners in improv will actively support whatever you say or do, and that you will do the same for them, you create a safe space for a scene to unfold. Doing improv requires courage, optimism, and a trusting playfulness that is willing to go with the flow and allow creativity to flourish.

Saying no awakens the inner censor, the critic who wants to control through correction, perfection, and expectations. It's the ego trying to control the show. But saying "yes" instead of "no" bypasses the critical, controlling perfectionist, and leaves the door open for the unexpected to enter the scene.

As in improv theater, so in improvising a life. Saying yes can open the door to creative adventures, new opportunities, and unexpected options. One way to say yes to life (and to God) is to practice affirmative prayer. Affirmative prayer is like being God's improv partner. You keep saying yes to the universal flow and continually co-create your experience of reality with God. (Julia Cameron suggests that if the God word bothers you, consider it to be an acronym for Good Orderly Direction.)

You can start with simple affirmations. And you can create a personal prayer of affirmation. First, take a deep breath and let go of all negative thoughts and fears. Next, recognize that God is the source of all good. Remember that you are connected to and a part of the source of good, and that a power greater than you loves and guides you. Visualize what you desire and speak words in the present tense that affirm that it is already yours. Use your imagination to picture and feel what it is like to live in that new reality. Then thank God and release your prayer to the infinite field of creative energy. Trust that God accomplishes this in ways you cannot yet imagine. Trust that it is so.

Here's a sample to give you an idea of how you can create an affirmative prayer:

Relax: Take a deep breath. Now let it out, letting go of fear, worry, and negative thoughts.

Recognize: God is here and is the infinite source of all good, and is the source of all my good.

Relationship: I am connected to and part of the infinite quantum field of possibilities. I am one with and connected to God.

Realize: There is that within me which knows what to do and I clearly see the good I desire. I affirm that it is already so and I picture it with joy. As it becomes more real in my heart and mind, this good is realized in material manifestation.

Rejoice: I thank God that what I desire is coming about under grace in perfect order and divine timing.

Release: I release this prayer to do its good and perfect work. And so it is.

Our intentions are our true prayers, and they are fueled
by the fire of our focused attention.

—MARY COX GARNER

Vigilance and focus are essentially the same activity
and both are essentially the same as prayer.
We align ourselves with truth through thought.
Thus, every thought becomes a prayer.

—VERNON M. SYLVEST, M.D.

Therefore I tell you, whatever you ask for in prayer,
believe that you have received it, and it will be yours.

—MARK 11:24 (NIV)

The new physics says, in effect,
that it is impossible not to be involved.

—LYALL WATSON

- I have the power to receive great abundance.
- I have the power to create great abundance.
- I know that I exist in a quantum field of limitless possibilities and that Infinite Good is right where I am and active in my experience.
- I embrace new thoughts, new ideas, and divine wisdom.
- I know that divine strength, energy, and power flow through me out into all I think, say, or do.
- The life of the Spirit is my life. The joy of the Lord is my strength.
- I am a channel for God's abundant love and it flows through me out into the world.
- Knowing that God is the great Giver, I accept God's gifts, and I myself become a giver and a gift to life.
- I see the good in every person and every event.
- I live free of fear for God is my ultimate source of good.
- I experience God's presence and peace at the center of my being.
- I am filled with joy and gratitude. I thank God for the gift of life.

GIVING THANKS

Gratitude unlocks the fullness of life.
It turns what we have into enough, and more.
It turns denial into acceptance, chaos to order, confusion to clarity.
It can turn a meal into a feast, a house into home, a stranger into a friend.
Gratitude makes sense of our past, brings peace for today,
and creates a vision for tomorrow.

—MELODY BEATTIE

One of the easiest ways to cultivate inner simplicity is to practice gratitude. By giving thanks for what we receive, we encourage the universe to shower even more of the good things of life upon us. We come to realize that we are rich in the things that count. Here are more joyful simplicities to give thanks for:

. . . sunset views

. . . making something with your own two hands

. . . a couple celebrating a golden wedding anniversary

. . . newlyweds in love, so young and beautiful it makes your heart ache

. . . voices singing in harmony

. . . visionary leaders who love and serve life

. . . fresh starts and new beginnings

. . . a full moon rising in the east

. . . the innocent eyes of a child

. . . a goal achieved

. . . an unexpected compliment

. . . a good "bad" joke—so bad you can't help laughing

. . . turtles sunning on a log and frogs croaking in a bog

. . . a peaceful neighborhood

. . . enjoying a good time after surviving tough times

. . . elders' wisdom and stories

. . . good manners

. . . hands open to give and to receive

. . . feeling pretty in pink

. . . sappy old movies with happy endings

. . . chocolate in almost any form

. . . butterflies in the sunlight

. . . national parks, state parks, local parks

. . . friendly conversation

. . . a clean restroom

. . . exercise class

. . . a brand new lipstick

. . . small towns with one stoplight

. . . the lights of home in the distance

. . . a well-watered garden

. . . a sigh of relief

. . . a trustworthy mechanic

. . . a hand to hold

. . . a partner to dance with

. . . someone you can depend on

All we have in life is what we notice.

—RICHARD BAKER-ROSHI

Gratitude is the heart's memory.

—FRENCH PROVERB

Blessed are those who can give without remembering
and take without forgetting.

—ELIZABETH BIBESCO

Actually, I don't have a sense of needing anything personally. I've learned by now to be quite content whatever my circumstances. I'm just as happy with little as with much, with much as with little. I've found the recipe for being happy whether full or hungry, hands full or hands empty. Whatever I am, wherever I am, I can make it through anything in the One who makes me who I am.

—PHILIPPIANS 4:11-13 (THE MESSAGE)

Let us rise up and be thankful,
for if we didn't learn a lot today, at least we learned a little,
and if we didn't learn a little,
at least we didn't get sick,
and if we got sick, at least we didn't die,
so, let us all be thankful.

—BUDDHA

FOR THE HIGHEST GOOD OF ALL

If we are to go forward, we must go back and rediscover those precious values: that all reality hinges on moral foundations and that all reality has spiritual control.

—MARTIN LUTHER KING, JR.

The art of simplicity is not only about things and experiences, it's about the choices you make and how you cultivate character. The old fashioned virtues have been neglected, but they are timeless essentials for a fulfilling life. You know how complex life can get when you procrastinate so long that a neglected problem takes on a life of its own. Suddenly the leak has become a flood, the pile of paper an avalanche inundating your desk, the little white lie turns into a complicated attempt to remember the stories you told. Sometimes the difficult choices turn out to be the simplest choices of all.

The choices and attitudes that make life simpler and easier are ones of character and integrity. Because you choose to cultivate character, honor your responsibilities, and believe in your own potential for good, you become a blessing to everyone around you. You become a channel for good in this world, fulfilling your potential and your calling in ways that expand ever outward. If, as some physicists believe, the movement of a butterfly wing can be the genesis of a storm on the other side of the globe, then the simplest choices for or against integrity, honesty, and love can have a more mighty impact on this world than you can imagine.

They are the real lovers of God,
Who feel others' sorrow as their own.
When they perform selfless service,
They are humble servants of the Lord.
Respecting all, despising none,
They are pure in thought, word, and deed.

—NARSINHA MEHTA

Let this list be a reminder of the kind of choices you want to make, the kind of character and habits you wish to cultivate, and the kind of attitude you want to have toward life.

. . . knowing that you can make a difference wherever you are

. . . giving thanks for every blessing

. . . believing the best instead of the worst

. . . being open to new ideas

. . . taking responsibility for your choices

. . . committing random acts of kindness

. . . changing direction when you realize you've been going down the wrong path

. . . taking time to pray and listen to God

. . . lending a helping hand

. . . encouraging one another

. . . celebrating the differences and affirming others' choices

. . . listening with your heart

. . . learning something new

. . . doing the best you can do with what you have

. . . seeing everything and everyone in the light of love

. . . enjoying a good laugh at yourself when you take yourself too seriously

. . . being fully present in the moment

. . . refusing to grumble or complain or blame

. . . working at something with your whole heart

. . . practicing kindness and consideration

. . . choosing generosity over fear and greed

. . . following through instead of procrastinating

. . . balancing "doing" and "being"

. . . doing the job right the first time

. . . taking pride in your work

. . . moving beyond your comfort zone

. . . trusting God

. . . honoring the dignity of every human being

. . . making room to include everyone in the circle

. . . doing your part to make a contribution to the good of the world

. . . honoring the sacred in life

. . . praising freely

. . . serving the highest good of all

I slept and dreamt that life was joy
I awoke and saw that life was service
I acted and behold, service was joy.

—RABINDRANATH TAGORE

There is no higher religion than human service.
To work for the common good is the greatest creed.

—ALBERT SCHWEITZER

What will matter most to us, upon deeper reflection,
is the quality of experience we create in the world,
not the quantity of the results.

—PETER BLOCK

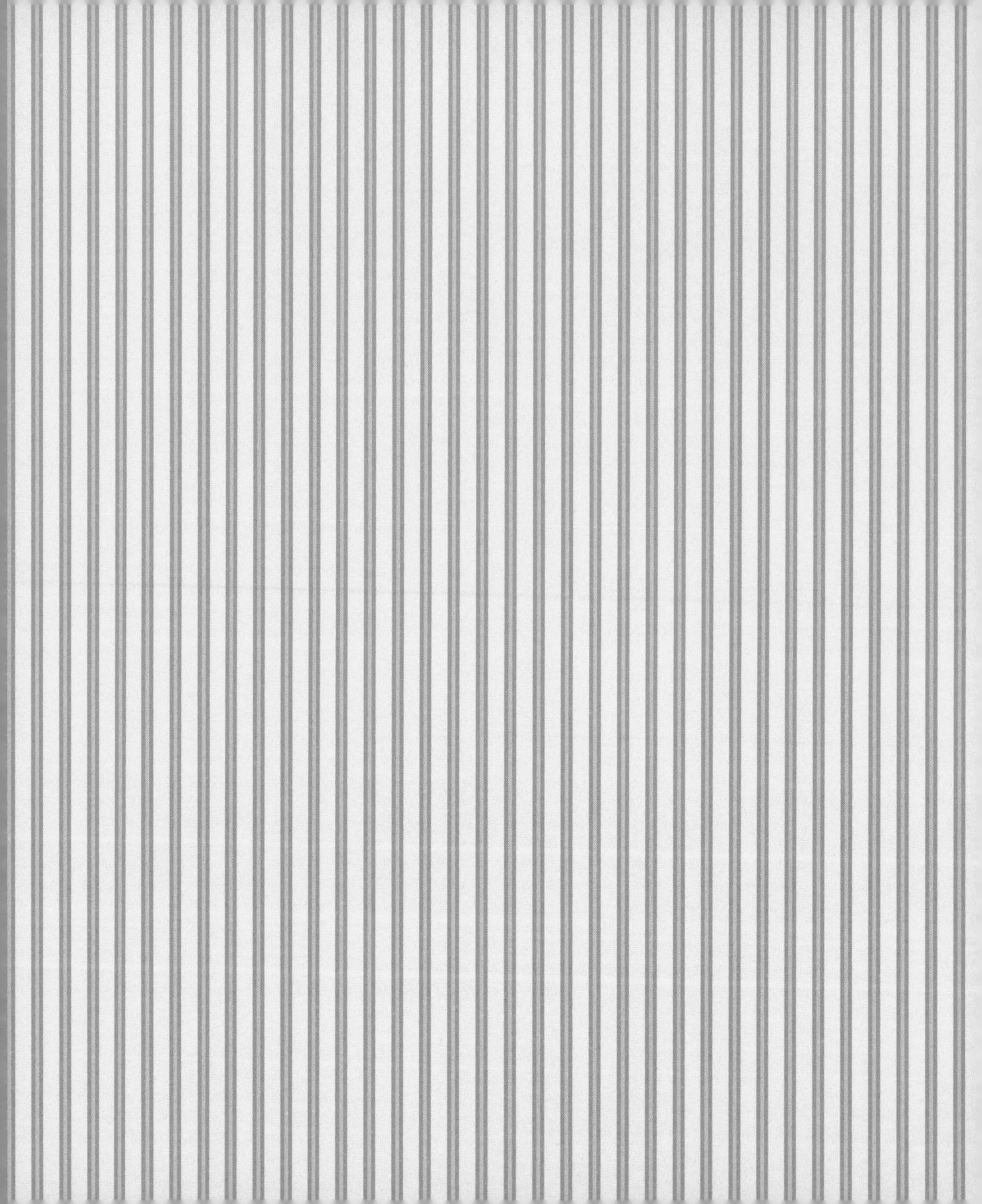

Dare to Dream

I strongly feel that death is actually a small concern compared to the living dead, who have not fulfilled their dreams or who have not been true to themselves. Live a life for which you can be thankful.

—PATCH ADAMS

WE ARE THE FUTURE

Our aspirations are our possibilities.

—SAMUEL JOHNSON

Clearing the inner clutter and freeing ourselves from past patterns that would hold us back is the beginning of liberty. But it is only a beginning. We are the ones we have been waiting for, and it is up to us to cultivate our potential for greatness and offer our gifts to the world. If we have emptied ourselves of prejudice, anger, and fear, then we can be filled with the love of God. We can be the hands of the Divine reaching out to bring a cup of cold water and a touch of grace to a hurting world. We can be the dreamers who make a more lovely and equitable world a reality. And with God's help, we will.

Whatever you can do or dream you can, begin it;
Boldness has genius, power, and magic in it.

—GOETHE

We can't take any credit for our talents.
It's how we use them that counts.

—MADELEINE L'ENGLE

When I look into the future, it's so bright it burns my eyes.

—OPRAH WINFREY

The Great Creator lives within each of us.
All of us contain a divine, expressive spark, a creative candle
intended to light our path and that of our fellows.

—JULIA CAMERON

We are the heroes of our own story.

—MARY MCCARTHY

Until you make peace with who you are,
you'll never be content with what you have.

—DORIS MORTMAN

The well of Providence is deep.
It's the buckets we bring to it that are small.

—MARY WEBB

Always be a first-rate version of yourself,
instead of a second-rate version of somebody else.

—JUDY GARLAND

I desire to create a world that will solve for others
what I have struggled with so much of my life.

—PETER BLOCK

The cornerstone of effective leadership is self mastery . . .
And the surest route to self mastery is spiritual practice.
Time spent in peaceful reflection or mindful meditation
clarifies thought, sharpens intuition, and curbs unhealthy instincts.

—PATRICIA ABURDENE

Here is a simple, rule-of-thumb guide for behavior:
Ask yourself what you want people to do for you, then grab the initiative
and do it for them. Add up God's Law and Prophets and this is what you get.

—MATTHEW 7:12 (THE MESSAGE)

Everything in the universe is related; we are all connected;
from stardust to human flesh, we vibrate with the same elements of the universe.
The web of life is infused by spirit, and each one of us has the power
to use that creative energy to manifest our potential.

—RUDOLFO ANAYA

THE GOLDEN SPIRAL

"For I know the plans I have for you," declares the Lord, "plans to prosper you and not to harm you, plans to give you a hope and a future."

—JEREMIAH 29:11 (NIV)

I remember the first time I read Oliver Wendell Holmes' poem, "The Chambered Nautilus." It was in a sea shell museum in Port Gamble, Washington. Mounted on the wall above the poem was a halved chambered nautilus shell, revealing the pearly interior spiral of that remarkable denizen of the deep. In a galaxy whorl of rainbow pearl, it marked the ever-spiraling stairway of growth as the creature became larger and larger. The life history of the chambered nautilus lay open and clear in the discarded shell. Once it had danced in beautiful majesty in the waters of the sea, but now only its empty shell reminded me of the living form which once inhabited its smooth chambers. And the poem took me on a soulful journey, showing me a picture of my own ever-evolving life.

We are great mysteries, living in the sea of life. Our lives follow a golden spiral of evolution—infant, child, adolescent, adult, middle age, old age.

There is that within our bodies which follows its own timetable of growth, change, and aging. We eat and food becomes part of our bodies, yet we still don't understand how food is transformed into a thought. Our bodies are the vessels through which we experience and interact with life, and our souls grow even as bodies age and die. Something greater within knows that the entire process is essential to this journey of life. Each experience, good and bad, becomes a part of our soul's evolution and transformation.

As the ebb and flow of tides of change wash through us, we can choose growth and expansion, or we can cling to the old ways of thinking and being. Still, even when we choose to cling, life itself changes around us, and we find that trying to stop the evolution of our souls is the way of death. If we choose to seek and embrace the changes, to ride the tides and trust a Higher Power that is both within and without, we co-create our destinies and become more than we ever dreamed we would be.

In fractals, nature's choice creates a continuous feedback loop. For us, each choice creates a spiral, a feedback loop that replicates itself again and again. A positive choice begins a spiral upward, and a negative choice spirals down. The power lies in this moment, this choice. At the intersection of here and now lies the opportunity to begin a new and happier pattern by making a different choice. We can take the high road and reach for our inner greatness.

We will see our positive choice amplified over time into a transformed life; a life with the potential to turn chaos into beauty and order.

Simplicity is relaxing into the stream of the life force, riding its currents to an unimagined destination, allowing the tides and seasons to make their mark on our souls, releasing that which no longer serves us to embrace a higher and more expansive good. We learn to trust the deeper wisdom of God and to make choices that amplify that trust. We surrender our own limited agendas to become co-creators with God.

May the wisdom of this poem remind you of your own potential for greatness and encourage you to trust that everything you need is already available to you and within you. May you know an ever-expanding goodness and come to realize that in God's eyes you are already whole, perfect, and complete. Every failure and every success, every lesson learned, every experience of beauty and despair, everything you've lost or loved—all these are essential for your spiritual evolution. May you learn how to tap the power within by making room for greater and greater good to enter your life. May you catch a glimpse of who you are in God's eyes so that you may aspire to become all you are meant to be. And may you fulfill your highest destiny as you travel life's golden spiral of growth and service.

The Chambered Nautilus

BY OLIVER WENDELL HOLMES (1809-1894)

This is the ship of pearl, which, poets feign,
Sail the unshadowed main,—
The venturous bark that flings
On the sweet summer wind its purple wings
In gulfs enchanted, where the Siren sings,
And coral reefs lie bare,
Where the cold sea-maids rise to sun their streaming hair.

Its webs of living gauze no more unfurl;
Wrecked is the ship of pearl!
And every chambered cell,
Where its dim dreaming life was wont to dwell,
As the frail tenant shaped his growing shell,
Before thee lies revealed,—
Its irised ceiling rent, it sunless crypt unsealed!

Year after year beheld the silent toil
  That spread his lustrous coil:
  Still, as the spiral grew,
He left the past year's dwelling for the new,
Stole with soft step its shining archway through,
  Built up its idle door,
Stretched in his last-found home, and knew the old no more.

Thanks for the heavenly message brought by thee,
  Child of the wandering sea,
  Cast from her lap, forlorn!
From thy dead lips a clearer note is born
Than ever Triton blew from wreathéd horn!
  While on mine ear it rings,
Through the deep caves of thought I hear a voice that sings:—

Build thee more stately mansions, O my soul,
  As the swift seasons roll!
  Leave thy low-vaulted past!
Let each new temple, nobler than the last,
Shut thee from heaven with a dome more vast,
  Till thou at length are free,
Leaving thine outgrown shell by life's unresting sea!

resources

SIMPLICITY

The Simple Living Guide, Janet Luhrs. (Broadway Books, 1997.)

Living the Simple Life: A Guide to Scaling Down and Enjoying More, Elaine St. James. (Hyperion, 1998.)

Making Choices: Discover the Joy in Living the Life You Want to Lead,

Alexandra Stoddard. (Avon Books, 1994.)

Elegant Choices, Healing Choices: Finding Grace and Wholeness in Everything We Choose, Marsha Sinetar. (Paulist Press, 1988.)

Simple Abundance: A Daybook of Comfort and Joy, Sarah Ban Breathnach. (Warner Books, 1995.)

FINANCES AND PROSPERITY

The Energy of Money, Maria Nemeth, Ph.D. (Ballantine Wellspring, 1997.)

The Nine Steps to Financial Freedom, Suze Orman. (Crown Publishers, 1997.)

Money Drunk Money Sober: 90 Days to Financial Freedom, Julia Cameron and Mark Bryan. (Ballantine Wellspring, 1992.)

Rich Dad Poor Dad, Robert T. Kiyosaki. (Warner Business Books, 1997.) Or visit www.richdad.com

How to Get Out of Debt, Stay Out of Debt, and Live Prosperously, Jerrold Mundis. (Bantam Books, 1998.)

Earn What You Deserve: How to Stop Underearning and Start Thriving, Jerrold Mundis. (Bantam Books, 1995.

Edwene Gaines Seminars
For information, call (256) 635-1377, or visit www.prosperityproducts.com.

WONDERFUL WOMEN

Lit From Within: Tending Your Soul for Lifelong Beauty, Victoria Moran. (HarperCollins, 2001.)

Women's Bodies, Women's Wisdom: Creating Physical and Emotional Health and Healing, Christiane Northrup, M.D. (Bantam Books, 1994.)

The Cloister Walk, Kathleen Norris. (Riverhead Books, 1996.)

Entre Nous: A Woman's Guide to Finding Her Inner French Girl, Debra Ollivier. (St. Martin's Griffin, 2003.)

The Dance of the Dissident Daughter: A Woman's Journey from Christian Tradition to the Sacred Feminine, Sue Monk Kidd. (HarperSanFrancisco, 1996.)

Prayer Is a Place: America's Religious Landscape Observed, Phyllis Tickle. (Doubleday, 2005.)

CREATIVITY

Walking on Water: Reflections on Faith and Art. Madeleine L'Engle. (Bantam Books, 1982.)

The Artist's Way: A Course in Discovering and Recovering Your Creative Self (1992), *The Vein of Gold: A Journey to Your Creative Heart* (1996), *Walking in This World: The Practical Art of Creativity* (2002), Julia Cameron. (Jeremy P. Tarcher/Putnam Publishing.)

Coaching the Artist Within, Eric Maisel. (New World Library, 2005.)

Affirmations for Artists, Eric Maisel. (Jeremy P. Tarcher/Putnam Publishing, 1996.)

Improv Wisdom: Don't Prepare, Just Show Up, Patricia Ryan Madson. (Bell Tower, 2005.)

Trust the Process: An Artist's Guide to Letting Go, Shaun McNiff. (Shambala, 1998.)

Your Heart's Desire: Instructions for Creating the Life You Really Want,

Sonia Choquette. (Three Rivers Press, 1997.)

Creating an Imaginative Life, Michael Jones. (Conari Press, 1995.)

Creative Ideas: A Spiritual Compass for Personal Expression, Ernest Holmes. (Science of Mind Publishing, 1973, 2004.)

Crossing the Unknown Sea: Work as a Pilgrimage of Identity, David Whyte. (Riverhead Books, 2001.)

Having It All: Body, Mind, Heart, and Spirit Together Again, Phil Porter with Cynthia Winton-Henry. (Body Wisdom, Inc., 1997.) From the creators of InterPlay.

What the Body Wants, Cynthia Winton-Henry with Phil Porter. (Northstone Publishing, 2004.) From the creators of InterPlay. For information about InterPlay®, visit www.interplay.org.

INTUITIVE MIND/HOLISTIC BODY

Yoga Mind, Body, and Spirit: A Return to Wholeness, Donna Farhi. (Henry Holt and Company, 2000.)

Bringing Yoga to Life: The Everyday Practice of Enlightened Living, Donna Farhi. (HarperSanFrancisco, 2003.)

Meditations from the Mat: Daily Reflections on the Path of Yoga, Rolf Gates and Katrina Kenison. (Anchor Books, 2002.)

Divining the Body: Reclaim the Holiness of Your Physical Self, Jan Phillips. (Skylight Paths, 2005.)

The Complete Idiot's Guide to Making Money Through Intuition, Nancy Rosanoff. (Alpha Books, 1999.)

Trust Your Vibes: Secret Tools for Six-Sensory Living, Sonia Choquette. (Hay House, 2004.)

Positive Energy, Judith Orloff. (Three Rivers Press, 2004.)

Conscious Breathing: How Shamanic Breathwork Can Transform Your Life, Joy Manné. (North Atlantic Books, 2004.)

The Spiritual Dimension of Therapeutic Touch, Dora Kunz with Dolores Krieger, Ph.D., R.N. (Bear & Company, 2004.)

For more information on Healing Touch, visit www.healingtouch.net.

Vibrational Medicine, Richard Gerber, M.D. (Bear & Company, 2001.)

Journey to Freedom: 13 Quantum Leaps for the Soul, Leslie Kenton. (Thorsons, 1998.)

Soulcraft: Crossing into the Mysteries of Nature and Psyche, Bill Plotkin. (New World Library, 2003.)

Healing Beyond the Body: Medicine and the Infinite Reach of the Mind, Larry Dossey, M.D. (Shambala, 2003.)

The Healer Within: Using Traditional Chinese Techniques to Release Your Body's Own Medicine, Roger Jahnke, O.M.D. (HarperSanFrancisco, 1997.)

The Healing Promise of Qi: Creating Extraordinary Wellness Through Qigong and Tai Chi, Roger Jahnke, O.M.D. (Contemporary Books, 2002.)

Belly Dancing: The Sensual Art of Energy and Spirit, Pina Coluccia, Anette Paffrath, Jean Püte. (Inner Traditions, 2005.)

Bellydancing for Fitness, Rania Androniki Bossonis. (Fair Winds Press, 2004.)

Grandmother's Secrets: The Ancient Rituals and Healing Power of Belly Dancing, Rosina-Fawzia Al-Rawi. (Interlink Books, 1999.)

The Nia Technique: The High-Powered Energizing Workout that Gives You a New Body and a New Life, Debbie Rosas and Carlos Rosas. (Broadway Books, 2004.)

Sacred Drumming, Steven Ash. (Sterling Publishing, 2001.)

For CDs and drum lessons by Ed Haggard, visit www.thelovedrums.com

CULTURAL VISIONARIES

The Cultural Creatives, Paul H. Ray, Ph.D. and Sherry Ruth Anderson, Ph.D. (Harmony Books, 2000.)

The Translucent Revolution: How People Just Like You Are Waking Up and Changing the World, Arjuna Ardagh. (New World Library, 2005.)

Megatrends 2010: The Rise of Conscious Capitalism, Patricia Aburdene. (Hampton Roads Publishing Company, 2005.)

Natural Capitalism: Creating the Next Industrial Revolution, Paul Hawken, Amory Lovins, L. Hunter Lovins. (Little, Brown, & Company, 1999.) Or visit www.naturalcapitalism.com.

Cradle to Cradle: Remaking the Way We Make Things, William McDonough and Michael Braungart. (Northpoint Press, 2002). Or visit www.McDonough.com.

The Answer to How is Yes: Acting on What Matters, Peter Block. (Berret-Koehler Publishers, 2002.)

SPIRITUAL VISIONARIES AND QUANTUM LEAPS

There's a Spiritual Answer to Every Problem, Wayne Dyer. (HarperCollins, 2001.)

The Spontaneous Fulfillment of Desire: Harnessing the Infinite Power of Coincidence, Deepak Chopra. (Harmony Books, 2003.)

Original Blessing: A Primer in Creation Spirituality, Matthew Fox. (Bear & Company, 1983.)

One River, Many Wells, Matthew Fox. (Jeremy P. Tarcher/Putnam, 2000.)

"Arise, My Love...": Mysticism for a New Era, William Johnston. (Orbis Books, 2000.)

A Course in Miracles, Foundation for Inner Peace (1992).

The Parables of the Kingdom, Robert Farrar Capon. (Eerdmans, 1985.)

The Science of Mind: A Philosophy, A Faith, A Way of Life, Ernest Holmes. (Jeremy P. Tarcher/Putnam, 1938.)

Joy's Way: A Map for the Transformational Journey, W. Brugh Joy, M.D. (Jeremy P. Tarcher/Putnam, 1979.)

Living Presence: A Sufi Way to Mindfulness and the Essential Self, Kabir Edmund Helminski. (Jeremy P. Tarcher/Putnam, 1992.)

Prayers of the Cosmos: Meditations on the Aramaic Words of Jesus, Neil Douglas-Klotz. (HarperSanFrancisco, 1999.)

Inner Christianity: A Guide to the Esoteric Tradition, Richard Smoley. (Shambala, 2002.)

Quantum Theology: Spiritual Implications of the New Physics, Diarmuid O'Murchu. (Crossroad Publishing, 2004.)

Living with Joy: Keys to Personal Power and Spiritual Transformation, Sanaya Roman. (H.J. Kramer, Inc., 1986.)

POETRY AND INSPIRATIONAL QUOTATIONS

Anthology of American Poetry, edited by George Gesner. (Crown/Avenal, 1983.)

Thinking Outside the Church: 110 Ways to Connect with Your Spiritual Nature, Jennifer Leigh Selig, Ph.D. (Andrews McMeel Publishers, 2004.)

The New Encyclopedia of Christian Quotes, compiled by Mark Water. (Baker Books, 2001.)

The Westminster Collection of Christian Quotes, compiled by Martin H. Manser. (Westminster John Know Press, 2001.)

Abounding Grace, edited with commentary by M. Scott Peck, M.D. (Andrews McMeel Publishers, 2000.)

The Treasure Chest. (HarperCollins, 1995.)

Zen Soup, Laurence G. Boldt. (Penguin Arkana, 1997.)

Golden Treasury of the Familiar, edited by Ralph L. Woods. (Crown/Avenal, 1980.)

Words I Wish I Wrote, compiled by Robert Fulghum. (HarperCollins, 1997.)

Spiritual RX: Prescriptions for Living a Meaningful Life, Frederic and Mary Ann Brussat. (Hyperion, 2000.)

Spiritual Literacy: Reading the Sacred in Everyday Life, Frederic and Mary Ann Brussat. (Scribner, 1996.)

The Fairview Guide to Positive Quotations, compiled by John Cook. (Fairview Press, 1996.)

MAGAZINES

Yes! A Journal of Positive Futures (www.YesMagazine.org)

Yoga Journal (www.YogaJournal.com)

Utne Reader (www.Utne.com)

Spirituality & Health (www.SpiritualityHealth.com)

Shift: At the Frontiers of Consciousness (The Journal of The Institute of Noetic Sciences, www.noetic.org)

Mary Jane's Farm (www.MaryJanesFarm.org)

Natural Home & Garden (www.NaturalHomeandGarden.org)

About the Author

Candy Paull is the author of *The Art of Simplicity*, *The Art of Abundance*, *The Art of Encouragement*, and *Christmas Abundance*.

A performing singer/songwriter, Candy has been a freelance writer specializing in marketing materials for book publishers, as well as being a buyer for bookstores and a marketing director for a small publisher.

Candy's open approach to spirituality draws insight and wisdom from many spiritual traditions, emphasizing that there is something within us that is trustworthy, whole, and wise. Instead of always trying to "fix" what is "broken" in our lives, she helps us experience the profound wholeness that lies at the center of the universe—and in our own human hearts. Through words and music, she takes complex concepts like grace, truth, goodness, beauty, sacredness, holiness, love, and mercy, and translates them into quiet wisdom that nourishes and enriches daily life.

Candy speaks, sings, and facilitates retreats that combine movement, music, readings, aromatherapy, and other healing modalities to help men and women reduce stress, enjoy a more creative and abundant life, and nurture spiritual growth by integrating body, mind, and spirit. She also speaks at conferences, seminars, and corporate events.

Candy Paull
P.O. Box 159276
Nashville, TN 37215
www.candypaull.com

Candy would like to thank Stephany Evans, Marisa Bulzone, Frank DeMarco, Donna Michael, Dr. Mitch Johnson, and Gerrie McDowell for their help and encouragement in the creation of this book.

Special thanks to my mother, Ruth Paull, whose unconditional love and generous support made this book possible. Mom, I can never fully repay the gifts you gave me, but I can make sure that the seeds of love you planted in me will grow, multiply, and bear fruit.

Credits